Transformation

Transformation

What is God doing and how do we join in?

Matt Bird

Copyright © 2017 Matt Bird

The moral right of the author has been asserted.

Apart from any fair dealing for the purposes of research or private study, or criticism or review, as permitted under the Copyright, Designs and Patents Act 1988, this publication may only be reproduced, stored or transmitted, in any form or by any means, with the prior permission in writing of the publishers, or in the case of reprographic reproduction in accordance with the terms of licences issued by the Copyright Licensing Agency. Enquiries concerning reproduction outside those terms should be sent to the publishers.

Matador
9 Priory Business Park,
Wistow Road, Kibworth Beauchamp,
Leicestershire. LE8 0RX
Tel: 0116 279 2299
Email: books@troubador.co.uk
Web: www.troubador.co.uk/matador
Twitter: @matadorbooks

ISBN 978 1788036 085

British Library Cataloguing in Publication Data.
A catalogue record for this book is available from the British Library.

Printed and bound in the UK by TJ International, Padstow, Cornwall
Typeset in 11pt Aldine401 BT by Troubador Publishing Ltd, Leicester, UK

Matador is an imprint of Troubador Publishing Ltd

To Jesus, thank you for not giving up on me.

To my wife Esther, thank you for enabling me to be who I am and do what I do.

To my children Joseph, Matilda and Reuben, thank you for inspiring me.

To my friends, thank you for living the great adventure of life together.

"This book is a call to something greater. Matt Bird confronts head on our self centred Christianity that has kept the Church so ineffective for so long. With recent and very relevant stories from around the globe you will be challenged that our role as Christians is to seek the welfare of our communities, and as we do that God is moving in new, fresh and exciting ways."
Letitia Shelton, OneChurch Toowoomba, Australia

"Matt Bird approaches the issue of societal transformation in an uncommon way. He first asks organically "What is God doing?" – and not: "What is the problem?" or "How can we achieve some-thing?" With a holistic biblical Kingdom of God perspective Matt takes a stunning tour of what the church in a city or nation is called to be today. The book highlights the indicators of transformational change that will challenge you to join the movement of God's spirit just where he has positioned you in daily life. Highly recommended, worth reading – and doing!"
Rev Axel Nelson, Together for Berlin, Germany

"Matt Bird's book is a practical and thoroughly Biblical approach to effective mission to bring change in today's world. The book is peppered with examples from his life and of others in the UK and around the world. It is well rounded and comes with sound practical suggestions for a holistic approach to mission. Matt's book lays a very good foundation for ministry in urban areas, which as an urban mission practitioner I find very helpful."
Viju Abraham, Mumbai Transformation Network, India

"Matt has committed his life to enabling the church to play its full role in society. The reflections in this book are not just good ideas, but have come with years of journey and experience. I highly recommend this book for anyone who wants to see the church being a force for good in society. An amazing book, written by an amazing person"
Bishop Mike Royal, Birmingham, UK

"With insight and discernment my good friend, Matt Bird, helpfully charts the journey which increasing numbers of people find themselves taking, in the UK and around the world. God is taking us to greater depths of unity, prayer, mission and mercy at city and town wide level. The world is noticing, too, as such commitment leads to greater favour and influence. Read this book to be encouraged and challenged."
Lloyd Cooke, Saltbox, Stoke-on-Trent, UK

"It is so refreshing and powerful when the 'Church' knows the times that they are in, and respond in aligning themselves to God's agenda for that season. Matt Bird does a brilliant job by answering the question "What is God doing and how do we join in?" All across the world there is a new revival of love, kindness and compassion in communities, cities and countries birthing inclusive transformation. A most timely contribution."
Alan Platt, Doxa Deo & City Changers Movement

"New models and approaches to social engagement are a must as the global Church seeks to regain a place of relevance and effectiveness. Remaining insular or relying on mere events or programs won't work by themselves. My friend, Matt Bird, presents challenging, inspiring and practical ways for us to achieve collective community transformation."
Guy Wasko, CityServe New York, US

"The realisation that the good news is not only about individual salvation but the holistic transformation of communities, cities and nations is growing worldwide. However, few are able to communicate the mission of God in clear, tangible, hope-giving and practical pathways that can easily be observed and followed as Matt Bird does in this book. I believe that Matt's book will inspire and mobilise many to pursue the transformation of their communities."
Piet Brinksma, Amsterdam Council of Christian Leaders, Netherlands

"When I first met Matt Bird in South Africa I immediately sensed that we have to connect with what he is accomplishing in the UK. Our cities in South Africa are going to benefit much from the initiative and creativity that Jesus has placed in him and the Cinnamon Network. We share the massive call of Micah 6:8 to see our cities transformed in their spiritual walk, social needs and levels of justice in society. May this book accelerate the faith, hope and love that the Church can bring in our world today!"
Jean Symons, Tshwane Pretoria, South Africa

"Matt Bird has given us a wonderful vista of what God is doing across the UK and around the world. This book inspires us to see the scope and extent of God's activity and is also very challenging as Matt encourages us to be involved as co-workers in this exciting mission. This book is packed with practical examples and penetrating questions. Read the book and walk this exciting journey to see even greater transformation."
Roger Sutton, Gather, UK

"Matt Bird is both widely travelled and deeply connected to practitioners in city transformation stories. Right now we are seeing the Father's dream and deep love for entire cities unfold. The Church is emerging, serving as one and amazing things are taking place! Matt's insights in this book will inform and inspire you to pursue God's purpose and plans for your town, your city, your place."
Rick Prosser, CityServe Newcastle, Australia

"In Transformation, Matt Bird provides a guided tour of key cities around the world and shines a light on where he sees God at work. He introduces the complex issues of today's city and how God's people are working together to respond. Before you are done reading this book, you can expect to hear God inviting you to join in."
Tim Day, Director of City Movement, Canada

"Matt Bird lives what he writes about. He writes from an authentic point of view and with great passion that fuels the words you're about to read. No one teaches it better, believes it more or engenders more enthusiasm than my friend Matt. Read it and live it."
Dean Curry, Tacoma, US

"Matt Bird has been gifted to not only discern but actively contribute to the move of God across our nation and beyond. In this book he beautifully shares his experiences and conclusions. His style is typically direct and challenging and he makes some bold statements with which I concur. I highly recommend this book to Christian leaders from all sectors of our society, including the Church."
Pastor Tani Omideyi, Together for a Harvest Liverpool, UK

"As God awakens the hearts of men and woman to see their cities transformed, Matt Bird's book Transformation becomes a wonderful tool to equip believers to engage and execute. Matt is a man determined to pursue God's dreams and purposes for a city transformation in all spheres of society. His commitment through genuine relationship to assist is authentic and selfless and I personally have been deeply challenged by his heart."
Chris Du Toit, City Story Durban, South Africa

"Every pastor and ministry leader who is seeking the peace and prosperity of their region should read this work. Matt Bird does an excellent job tangibly demonstrating Revelation 21:5 – "behold I am making all things new". If you believe that the local church is the hope of the world, this book is for you."
Edwin Copeland, Church United South Florida, US

"Any book by Matt Bird is likely to be worth reading. This little gem is no exception. I love his encouragement for us to find out what God is doing and join in – Holy energy – a brilliant concept. If we allow the home-spun wisdom of this book to guide us we are much more likely to live the life that God intended."
Gary Streeter MP, Chair of Christians in Parliament

"This new book by Matt Bird inspires and challenges us, individually and collectively, to demonstrate the gospel in our communities, workplaces, churches and homes. It succinctly and clearly covers much ground and should be read by anyone seeking to make a difference with their lives and with their faith. It is incredibly practical and a great missional resource for the church."
Prof Paul McCrone, Health Economics at Kings College, London

Contents

Foreword	xv
Introduction	xviii
1. De-Privatising Faith	1
2. God's Transformation Strategy	13
3. Stronger Together	22
4. Prayer Rising	32
5. A Force for Good	40
6. Cultural Change	49
7. Talking Jesus	60
8. Good Community	68
9. Participative Society	75
10. Numbers Speak Louder Than Words	83
11. Salt and Pepper	91
12. Distinctive Faiths	100
13. Outrageous Generosity	108
14. Unlikely Relationships	119
Conclusion	126
About the Author	131

Foreword

You're holding a quiet little book that tells the secret to changing the world.

Working as a Christian for the good of your community, it can often feel like lonely work. But none of us truly are alone. Just like the Holy Spirit empowered the Church in Acts 2 to turn Jerusalem upside down before spreading to the nations, we are each working as part of a movement. We are empowered by the same Spirit, called by the same God. That God is working not only to bring Good News and love to each individual, but to the cities, systems, and neighbourhoods that so deeply impact our lives. His love transforms.

Our mission of loving change has been the Christian call from the beginning of our faith. But the learning curve can be steep. The road can be arduous. We all have things to learn, strategies to hone, relationships to build, weaknesses to overcome. In a sense, community transformation is one massive group experiment. We look over the shoulders of others and ask, "What are you up to? Can we compare notes?"

As we walk and work alongside other believers, learning from each other is essential. Matt, in these pages, claims to be "just another guy". But I can assure you that his wisdom is anything but everyday. There are hard-earned lessons of faithful creativity and innovation here. Matt is worth listening to.

As many of us find ourselves seeking and encouraging a more "public" faith for the common good of our cities, we are all looking to others who are learning similar things about God, the city, and ministry strategy in order to steward our opportunities well. Matt's articulation of moving from a "self-focused" faith to truly letting light shine is inspiring. It may also feel familiar. We are, indeed, in a "revival of love", a term Matt uses to highlight the depth of the church and community partnerships that are bringing God's people together with the leaders and public servants of their locale.

Transformation is a whole package deal. When a life is turned upside down by God, everything that individual touches should be affected as well. Salvation sets us on a track of growth, connection, and work. A track of change. But how can we encourage that? How can we faithfully nourish and obey our call to work for "the city" (Jeremiah 29:7)?

It's all physics, really. Change requires movement, and movement needs energy. The "holy energy" that Matt writes of is no different than what propels the Gospel forward in our work here in Portland, Oregon. It's what we are witnessing in cities all around the world, flowing from that Acts 2 moment so many years ago. Such energy produces movements that are united, holistic, and sustainable. Or at least, they can be. We bear witness to that.

Read on to be encouraged and resourced for this calling. Look with Matt for the signs of God's work in this often-confusing world. Look for that holy energy, which is still turning hearts to Jesus, changing lives, and impacting cities. Look with him. Be attentive with him. Choose to join God, to make ourselves part of His big story, and bring His transformation power into the stories of our neighbourhoods, churches, cities, and nations.

God is at work. The only question left is whether we are willing to join Him in the effort.

Kevin Palau
President, Luis Palau Association, and author of
Unlikely: Setting Aside Our Differences To Live Out The Gospel

Introduction

Jesus gave them this answer: "Very truly I tell you, the Son can do nothing by himself; he can do only what he sees his Father doing, because whatever the Father does the Son also does. For the Father loves the Son and shows him all he does."
(John 5:19-20).

This book is about searching for the answer to a double-barreled question, "What is God doing and how do we join in?" Jesus lived by getting to know his Father and only doing what he saw him doing. So, if it was good enough for Jesus it is more than good enough for us.

Personally I feel life is too short, and moves too fast, to waste time, energy and resources coming up with our own mission and asking God to bless it in the hope that we might be successful. There are many great ideas out there, most of which come to nothing because God is not in them. Trust me, I've come up with a few myself – they were great ideas but not God ideas so they have gone nowhere. If we want to avoid unnecessary failure and maximise success – I certainly do – then the best approach is to identify what God is doing and find a way to be part of it, because God never fails.

God has been at work throughout human history and I believe this 'big story' can be explained in four simple episodes. Episode one is 'creation'. God created the world, he created humankind to be like him, he created us to have a relationship with him and have responsibility for looking after creation. The second episode is the 'fall'. This tells of our rebellion from God that causes brokenness in all our relationships; with him, with one another and with creation. Episode three is 'redemption'. It is how God reached out to restore these relationships and save us by ultimately sending his son Jesus Christ. Then the final episode is 'transformation'. It is how God is restoring and renewing all relationships to establish the Kingdom of God on earth as it is in heaven.

Sometimes as the Church we have been guilty of focusing on episodes two and three, of fall and redemption, at the cost of episodes one and four, of creation and transformation. This book is about understanding God's entire meta-narrative and finding our place within it today.

If we start with David soon after he was made King of Israel, we hear of tribes that came to offer their allegiance to him. The Bible says that the people of Issachar, 'understood the times and knew what Israel should do' (1 Chronicles 12:32). In just the same way we, as the people of God today, want to understand the times we are living in and know what we should do.

Sometime later when Israel was dispersed amongst the nations a Jew called Esther was chosen by King Xerxes to be his wife. There was a point when the Jewish people were threatened by genocide and Esther realised that her purpose was, 'for such a time as this' (Esther 4:14). Each of us is born for a reason and positioned at a time in history to help fulfil God's divine purposes.

Our challenge is to be attentive and sensitive to what God is doing at a particular time and ensure that we join him in it. Ecclesiastes says, 'There is a time for everything, and a season for every activity under the heavens: a time to be born and a time to die, a time to plant and a time to uproot, a time to kill and a time to heal, a time to tear down and a time to build, a time to weep and a time to laugh, a time to mourn and a time to dance, a time to scatter stones and a time to gather them, a time to embrace and a time to refrain from embracing, a time to search and a time to give up, a time to keep and a time to throw away, a time to tear and a time to mend, a time to be silent and a time to speak, a time to love and a time to hate, a time for war and a time for peace' (Ecclesiastes 3:1-8).

God's mission in the world and his work in our lives can involve times of painful pruning as well as times of growth and new life. Jesus said, "My Father is the gardener. He cuts off every branch joined to me that does not bear fruit. He trims every branch that does bear fruit. Then it will bear even more fruit" (John 15:1-2). We can be comforted by the knowledge that God only prunes who and what he cares about and in turn wants to grow. The key is to discern between what is decaying towards death, which we should walk away from, and what is being pruned for new life and growth which we should lean into and be part of.

One of the main ways of discerning what God is doing in our own lives as well as our communities, cities and countries is to look for what I call holy energy. When we see, hear and experience an unusual sense of the life of God that is a place of holy energy. Where there is such divine activity we can choose to join in by deploying our God-given time, energy and resources in that direction also.

This book is not presenting a strategy, methodology or blue print for community, city and country transformation. I'm just another guy, who is passionate about following Jesus, offering my perspective on the incredibly exciting ways that I see God at work in his world. My prayer is that this book helps you be more attentive to understanding the times we are living in and how you might more closely journey and join in with God's big story.

Matt Bird

matt@mattbirdspeaker.com
www.mattbirdspeaker.com

www.youtube.com/mattbirdspeaker
www.facebook.com/mattbirdspeaker
www.instagram.com/mattbirdspeaker
www.twitter.com/mattbirdspeaker

1

De-Privatising Faith

You are the light of the world. A town built on a hill cannot be hidden. Neither do people light a lamp and put it under a bowl. Instead they put it on its stand, and it gives light to everyone in the house. In the same way, let your light shine before others, that they may see your good deeds and glorify your Father in heaven.
(Matthew 5:14-16)

What is God doing?

One of the greatest obstacles to community, city and country transformation is the privatisation of faith. Faith in Jesus is profoundly personal, but it was never meant to be private – it is a public faith that should benefit everyone.

God is giving his Church a fresh confidence and courage to express faith in the public square. It's a faith that outworks itself in the civic soul, strategy and structures of our communities, cities and countries for the benefit of all people.

A few years ago I reached a point in my faith where things simply couldn't continue in the same way. I had attended so many Christian conferences, read so many Christian books and purchased every possible Christian product. I felt a little like you do when you've eaten too much Christmas dinner or when you've bought the big super value bar of chocolate from the supermarket for a movie night and midway through the film you realise you've only got a couple of squares left and feel rather unwell. I felt that if I consumed any more Christian resources the unthinkable was going to happen. I know it sounds strange, but that is how I felt about my faith.

My faith had become self-centred, self-focused and self-indulgent. I had reduced my faith to a relationship between Jesus and me and a concerted effort to take as many people as I possibly could with me to heaven when I died. I sensed God was calling me to change my focus and de-privatise my faith; to take that which I had made private and to make it public.

Our faith in Jesus is a profoundly personal matter, but it is never meant to be a private matter. As Jesus said, "You are the light of the world. A city built on a hill cannot be hidden. Neither do people light a lamp and put it under a bowl. Instead they put it on its stand and it gives light to everyone in the house. In the same way let your light shine before others, that they may see your good deeds and glorify your Father in heaven." (Matthew 5:14-16). Real faith cannot be hidden; it is clear for all to see.

One of my first wobbly steps towards de-privatising my faith involved joining a political party. As often happens with memberships, such as at a church or a gym, I signed up for the badge and that was it. Then, after six months I decided to get out and do something, so I began by volunteering with my local political group one Saturday morning. After all, I'd leafleted and knocked on doors for Jesus, so surely I could do so for my political convictions.

All went well as I happily stuffed envelopes with political bumpf until, about ten minutes into my stint, I was asked to step into a side room. I had no idea what was coming and, little did I know, it would change my life. A kind local activist explained to me that a local authority election was to be held in a few months' time and that they still had a vacancy for a candidate. They took great care to explain that the seat was unwinnable and so they were merely looking for a 'paper candidate' who would be a name on the ballet paper. It doesn't look good if the party fails to put forward a full quota of candidates. So I agreed.

On the day of election, I turned up at 'the count', as it was affectionately called, which was held at the local town hall. The process took hours and so at about 1.30am when the Chief Executive finally took to the podium to announce who had been elected, I was agitatedly looking at my watch and willing him to hurry up so I could get home to bed. You cannot believe my surprise, nor that of my political party, when they reached my ward and announced that I had won!

It was rather a shock to the system to say the least, but what it did do was to kickstart the journey of de-privitasing my faith. I am still learning what it truly means to embrace faith in the public sphere. Sometimes my steps are strong and deliberate and sometimes they are weak and faltering – but it's all part of the adventure of faith that we are called to.

Christianity has often been reduced to a pietistic private matter between Jesus and individuals. This can result in high levels of church attendance, but minimal impact in the community and culture. This is why some USA states, despite having some of the highest levels of church attendance in the country, also have the highest levels of gun crime. It is why some African states, despite professing faith on a national level, have the highest levels of corruption. It is why the UK, despite having a rich and resourceful church, has communities with some of the highest levels of poverty in Europe.

Living out a public faith is not always easy, but it is essential, which is part of my motivation for setting up the charity Cinnamon Network. Cinnamon Network is part of the way I am working through my calling to de-privatise my faith and develop a potent public faith that is transformational. Cinnamon is focused on helping local churches build transforming relationships in their communities and develop a faith that is a force for good. It is when we embrace a public faith, rather than a private faith, that we discover God's power to transform communities, cities and countries.

There are so many very practical reasons why the Church is such a force for good in our communities. A report by New Philanthropy Capital called 'What a difference faith makes' highlights the strengths of faith-based organisations. The first strength is resilience. With an army of volunteers, great networks with other churches and the sheer fact they have a physical base, churches are strong and robust deliverers of community support. Secondly, the Church has a unique reach. Churches are well established in communities and, as a result, are often well-trusted. Their longevity and religious commitment adds to their perseverance which is essential in building effective community relationships.

When talking to civic leaders and organisations about what the Church does and can do in the community there can, however, be a little nervousness, particularly when it comes to exploring partnership and funding. In part this nervousness comes from organisations' concerns that as the Church we might only serve people who agree with our beliefs or those we are trying to persuade to agree with our faith. It's an understandable concern.

'What a difference faith makes' highlights a number of interesting issues and misconceptions facing faith-based organisations: 'A challenge of faith-based charities is the lack of understanding of faith', 'concerns around proselytising can cause problems for faith-based charities, with beneficiaries and funders' and 'sometimes there is a perception that faith-based charities are only there to help those of their own faith. This can cause problems for faith-based charities as beneficiaries may not seek them out and funders may not want to fund them.' The good news is, that, and I quote from New Philanthropy Capital, 'We found this perception is generally unfounded'. Faith-based groups are not biased, insular clubs, but we have to work hard to demonstrate that.

Civic leaders don't always know how to express these concerns and are sometimes nervous about doing so. As a result, apprehension can exist under the surface and end up prejudicing decisions regarding funding. So, to nip these concerns in the bud, I like to address them early to try and prevent them from sabotaging a potential partnership. I explain that Cinnamon is 'faith based not faith biased' that we are motivated by Jesus' love (they can cringe at this point) but that we serve people of all faiths and none, and then they look relieved.

Civic leaders know the Church is motivated by faith so there is no point trying to hide it. The question is not, "As you serve people will you talk about Jesus?" but more, "As you serve people how will you talk about Jesus?" Of course we are going to talk about Jesus but are we going to do that in a way that fully respects others and is led by their interest and enquiry rather than us forcibly pushing our faith upon others as we seek to argue them around?

In my early years of faith, I expressed my passion for Jesus by trying to refute people's objections to my faith. I naively thought I could 'persuade' them into the Kingdom of God. As years passed I learnt that it is the Holy Spirit who works in people's lives to lead them to God. It's my role to introduce them, but it's the Holy Spirit who does the transformation. This was, in fact, a very freeing realisation. I no longer felt the need to push my faith on anyone, so I could spend more energy on simply loving them. In my subsequent experience, I've come to understand that this is what civic leaders need to be assured about.

Everyone comes to charity, philanthropy and public service with motives. I'm of the view that it's best to be up front about them. I was once facilitating a meeting between the chief executive of a local authority, a police commander and a group of church leaders. We had been discussing austerity and the impact on local government and police services. One of the church leaders turned to the two civic leaders and said, "When we do what we do in communities and the opportunity arises we will talk about Jesus who is the reason for what we do. Is that a problem to us working together?" There was a palpable silence and then the chief executive said, "We are so desperate we will work with anyone," and everyone laughed.

The chief executive was only partly joking; austerity means that local governments, police and other agencies are desperate to work with partners who can make a difference. As they say, necessity is the mother of invention. If austerity has brought any benefit it is the openness of statutory organisations to consider working with local churches in ways they historically wouldn't have. I have heard some people complain that statutory organisations are taking advantage of the Church, in a sense it doesn't matter, what matters is that they are helping the Church do what the Bible tells us to do, so who cares!

It's worth pausing for a moment to take inspiration from Jeremiah. Now Jeremiah is probably one of the most depressing books in the Bible, it's certainly not one to read from cover to cover in one sitting if you are feeling a little low. The prophet Jeremiah had the tough job of sharing a message of doom and gloom with Israel. He had to inform them that they were going to be defeated by their enemy. When the city of Israel was finally overcome by the Babylonians, the leaders were exiled to live in Babylon and God told the exiled Israelites to make the city their home; to build homes, develop businesses, marry one another and have children. He also instructed them to "seek the peace and prosperity of the city" (Jeremiah 29:5-7).

If Israel, at a time of crisis and transition, should pursue the peace and prosperity of their enemies' capital Babylon, how much more should we pursue the peace and prosperity of the cities that we call home. The thing is, we can only do that when we have de-privatised our faith and decided that it is good news not just for ourselves but for everyone.

The great hope of Jeremiah is that if we pursue the peace and prosperity of the city in which we live then we can put concerns for our future in God's hands, "For I know the plans I have for you, plans to prosper you and not to harm you, plans to give you hope and a future" (Jeremiah 29:11). This is a frequently quoted passage and one that is a source of great comfort to many. But, as a good friend once pointed out to me, the promise of a future full of hope is conditional on us first blessing our community in which we live.

There is a myriad of ways to pursue the peace and prosperity of the city. I have told you the story of how I came to be a local government councillor. There are many followers of Jesus all around the world who have been called into local government, either as elected officials or as civil servants. We need more and more people to hear this call if we are to transform the policies and structures of our communities.

The other way we can build peace and prosperity is to build relationships with local political leaders and ask them what their greatest challenges are and then do something to help. This is what Billy Kennedy and other church leaders did in Southampton when the local authority had to cut millions of pounds from their budget. They met with the Director of Children's Services and asked what their key priorities were and how the church could help. The director highlighted three areas: fostering and adoption, youth work, and provision for under-fives. In response, the churches met and ran a campaign to recruit forty foster families to meet the immediate challenge faced by the city council. They researched church based youth work and discovered that churches employed seventeen youth workers who then began working more closely with the local authority. They also discovered that the churches ran thirty-eight parent and toddler groups, so the city council ran a training course to help them understand the pressing social needs and to open up their groups to the wider community. Out of this conversation, Love Southampton was formed and exists today as a conduit for liaison between the churches and city council.

There are many other great examples across the world. Church leaders meeting across Portland, Oregon in the US became convicted that there was a gap between the life of the Church and the life of the city. This was exacerbated by the fact that the city of Portland prides itself on being one of the most socially liberal in the US – for example, Oregon was one of the first states to conduct a same sex marriage ceremony and it hosts an annual naked bike ride – whilst the Church is socially as well as theologically conservative.

So civic leaders and church leaders were naturally suspicious of each other. Kevin Palau and a group of other church leaders met with Mayor Sam Adams, and apologised for their lack of involvement in the life of the city and asked what they could do to serve the people who live there. Note that there was no mention of changing opinions, challenging policy or revolutionising behaviour, it was all about service. The following year more 10,000 church volunteers became involved in the life of the city offering to foster children, house the homeless and support the administration in countless other areas. At the end of the first year Mayor Sam Adams spoke in front of 40,000 people at a city churches festival to say "thank you and please don't stop". You'll be pleased to know they haven't.

Pressing into relationships with civic leaders is a powerful way of de-privatising our faith. We can start conversations that genuinely ask them about the challenges they face and discuss how we can help and support them. This is not rocket science, but it is not something that the Church always does.

Let's emancipate and liberate our faith from prison where it is locked up, controlled, constrained, and impotent to change the world. Let's de-privatise our faith to make Jesus meaningful at the heart of our communities, cities and countries to bring transformation.

How do we join in?

1. *Where are you on the continuum between private faith and public faith?*

2. *What could you do today that would de-privatise your faith further?*

3. *How well do you know the political leaders in your community, city or country? If you saw each other in the street, would you know each other by name and stop to have a conversation?*

4. *How well do civic leaders know you? If there was a crisis in the community would civic leaders ask you for help?*

5. *What are the greatest social needs your local, regional and national governments are currently facing and what is the Church doing about them?*

2

God's Transformation Strategy

God is love… Whoever claims to love God yet hates a brother or sister is a liar. For whoever does not love their brother and sister, whom they have seen, cannot love God, whom they have not seen. And he has given us this command: Anyone who loves God must also love their brother and sister.
(1 John 4:16b, 20-21)

What is God doing?

Over recent decades we have heard much about revival and there have been a number of hot spot 'destinations' where people who are passionate about revival have taken pilgrimage. We have also been presented with strategies and campaigns to achieve change, none of which have really come to much in terms of being transformational. God is passionate about revival and transformation. However, his strategy is simple but costly. It is a revival of love, kindness and relationships in homes and on the streets of our communities, cities and countries that brings transformation.

Roseto Valfortore is a small Italian village 100 miles southeast of Rome. Life was not easy for the community here, and they made a living for themselves through subsistence farming. In 1882, eleven of the community emigrated to the United States in search of a better life. They settled in Pennsylvania and in the years that followed hundreds of others from the community followed in their footsteps and they established Roseto Pennsylvania.

More recently, a local doctor was speaking to a visiting doctor called Stewart Wolf and mentioned that he had hardly ever seen a case of heart disease in a Rosetan patient under sixty-five years old. This dramatic revelation intrigued Dr. Wolf, so he began to research why this might be. Initially he thought the Rosetans' diet had something to do with it, but they ate at least us much fatty food and drank as much wine as patients in any other part of the United States. Then he thought it might be their active lifestyle and exercise, but again people were as overweight and obese as the general population, if not more so. He examined every possible factor including the genetics and local environment to try and explain the fact that the Rosetan death rate was 30-35% lower than that of the general population. He could find no cause.

As Dr. Wolf continued to get to know the community and understand what made them different, he realised that what marked this community out in contrast to others, was their social relationships. Families lived together inter-generationally, there were many civic organisations, a strong egalitarian ethos in the community and the life of the church had a transforming effect on the people. The answer to their good health and well-being was, in fact, the social structure, relationships and love the Rosetanss enjoyed.

Perhaps this should come as no surprise given recent research into the mental health of our nation. The Mental Health Foundation report 'Relationships in the 21st Century' published in 2016 states that, 'the influence of social relationships on the risk of death are comparable with well-established risk factors for mortality such as smoking and alcohol consumption and exceed the influence of other risk factors such as physical inactivity and obesity'. Social relationships are the oxygen of life – they lead to happier, healthier and longer lives.

God designed us to live in loving, supportive relationships, so it is no wonder that when we do so we live happier, healthier and longer as a result. Our God, is a God of relationships – three persons in one being. The Son loves the Father and the Father loves the Son, a love that sacrifices one for the other. The Holy Spirit continues the work that the Son began on Earth – work that the Son saw the Father doing. God is a God of love, relationship, community, sacrifice and preferment of the other. The Bible tells us that we are created in the image and likeness of God, so we are born for love, relationship, community, sacrifice and preferment of the other. We only become fully human, or fully who God made us to be, when we live in loving relationship with him and others.

Looking back on my own story, I now realise my home life was impoverished of relationships outside of our immediate family. I can remember only one occasion when I was allowed to bring a friend home from school to play. I can remember times when the doorbell rang my father would put the TV on mute and usher my mum, my sister and I to hide behind the sofa and pretend no-one was home. Later, I realised that this wasn't normal family behaviour. Those experiences and others that I grew up with hugely shaped my formative years and led me to lack self-confidence.

When I met a bunch of people who loved Jesus and were very open about their faith, I felt very uncomfortable. However, I was curious about what knowing Jesus meant, so I gave them, and then God, a chance and I've never looked back. Knowing that God not only loved me but also liked me was revolutionary. I began a journey of becoming confident in myself, in building relationships with other people and latterly standing on platforms speaking to tens of thousands of people. That's quite a change for the boy who would hide behind the sofa when the doorbell rang! Jesus has genuinely transformed my life.

It's not just a social transformation either; there is a cosmic alignment between the quality of our social relationships and our health and well-being. When Jesus was walking to Jerusalem he passed a village and heard ten lepers shouting at him from a distance for help. He immediately told them to go to the priest and as they went they were healed (Luke 17:11-19). At the time of Jesus, it was actually the priests who diagnosed leprosy by declaring people to be "unclean". Along with this 'diagnosis' also came spiritual and social exclusion, which is why Jesus told the lepers to go and show themselves to the Priest so he could declare them clean again.

Leprosy is a contagious disease and so lepers were shunned by society and forced to live in their own communes. This is why the lepers stood at a distance to shout for help, rather than approaching Jesus personally. Isolated in such communes lepers were unable to work, own businesses or interact with broader society driving them further into poverty and isolation. They were as poor as poor could be, being both socially and economically excluded. So to be loved and accepted by Jesus and then cleansed and healed from leprosy by him, as these ten men were, was totally transformational on so many different levels: physically, spiritually, socially and economically.

I believe this level of relational transformation is just as achievable today. Cinnamon Network makes it as easy as possible for local churches to build such transforming relationships in their communities. One of our unique approaches is that we find local church community projects that we think are outstanding and we incubate and support them through a process that enables them to package up what they do so that other local churches can replicate the same project.

In this way we drive best practice and save churches from having to reinvent the wheel. Cinnamon UK currently has a menu of more than thirty outstanding local church-based community projects that have been replicated by more than 3,500 other local churches, mobilising 56,000 church based volunteers and impacting 1.4 million community beneficiaries. Our work is far from done, but we are moving towards a revival of love and relationships. All the Cinnamon community projects provide a meaningful way for one human being to love, accept and care for another human and that is what transforms lives.

Motivation for engaging in and serving our communities is really important. I believe that if we are truly motivated by Jesus Christ then there should be no strings attached to what we do. We should not be primarily loving and serving because we want people to come to our church, but because we are expressing the loving and generous character and personality of God.

Romans (5:8) says, 'God has demonstrated his love to us in this, that whilst we were still sinners Christ died for us'. God has loved us unconditionally and so we should love others in the same way. Otherwise we are at risk of accepting God's love for ourselves on an unconditional basis and expressing God's love to others on a conditional basis. Of course, we would like people to come to Christ and come to Church, however we should love and serve them without an ulterior motive as an expression of God's generous love.

A community beneficiary once asked a church volunteer, "If I don't accept your Jesus will you still be my friend?" The answer to that question has to be 'yes' otherwise we are not loving with God's love. The amazing thing is that when we do love people unconditionally they do come to Christ and they do come to Church, but if we start with that motive people see straight through it. In the same way, we don't love and serve others to make God love us more, we love and serve because we are loved.

Loving unconditionally becomes a lot easier when we have a sober perspective rather than a self-righteous view of ourselves. This, combined with a high view of the dignity and worth of other people, is extremely powerful. Jesus said, "'Lord, when did we see you hungry or thirsty or a stranger or needing clothes or sick or in prison, and did not help you?' He will reply, 'Truly I tell you, whatever you did not do for one of the least of these, you did not do for me.'" (Matthew 25:44-45). When we find the image of Christ in other people, it becomes a lot easier to show them unconditional love, acceptance and service.

God's divine strategy for the transformation of communities, cities and countries is loving relationships; a genuine loving relationship with him, with one another as well as ourselves. When Jesus was asked by religious leaders about the greatest commandment, he replied, "Love the Lord your God with all your heart and with all your soul and with all your mind" and to "Love your neighbour as you love yourself" (Matthew 22:37-39). It is clear from what Jesus said that we cannot truly love other people until we love ourselves.

This actually poses a few problems. There are a few people who think of themselves more highly than they should, but most people I meet do not think of themselves highly enough. If inside, we are unaccepting and unforgiving of ourselves then we will not be able to fully accept and forgive others. Working on becoming the best possible version of our self is essential as we help other people become the best possible version of themselves also.

Practically we can do more to demonstrate the heart, character and personality of God by loving people and loving communities. Whether this is reaching out to our neighbours, the community around our church, our colleagues and customers at work, the civic leaders in our village, town or city or our countries' leadership, the key to people's hearts and minds is selflessness, acceptance, interest in and love of others.

It is God's sacrificial love demonstrated through his people that changes and transforms lives. Let's follow God's community, city and country transformation strategy and give ourselves to a highly costly revival of love and kindness!

How do we join in?

1. *What are the contexts in which God has called you to transform lives by loving people?*

2. *What boundaries do you tend to place on your love for others that God does not put on his love for you?*

3. *If you are to love people as God loves them, then what is it going to cost you?*

4. *How could you make changes in your life to have more time, energy and resources to show God's love and kindness to other people?*

5. *How can followers of Jesus across your city work together to bring about transformation?*

3

Stronger Together

My prayer is not for them alone. I pray also for those who will believe in me through their message, that all of them may be one, Father, just as you are in me and I am in you. May they also be in us so that the world may believe that you have sent me.
(John 17:20-21)

What is God doing?

For many years Church unity has been driven by national ecumenism and local fraternities of priests and pastors who meet because it's a good thing to do. God has however ignited a global grassroots, bottom up unity where church leaders of different colours, flavours and styles are finding one another and representing the Church together in their communities, cities or countries.

The way UK churches relate to one another has changed significantly in recent years. A couple of decades ago I can remember trying to get two groups of church leaders in a city to meet together, but they refused because one was theologically charismatic and the other theologically reformed. Another even stranger experience was in a different city when I was part of a joint churches initiative. We were discussing who would be a good guest speaker and one ambitious leader suggested inviting Billy Graham. One of the other pastors immediately explained that they would have a problem with that because he was theologically liberal. I didn't know whether to laugh or cry! Thankfully times have changed.

Over a number of years, I worked hard in my home community of Wimbledon in London to win the confidence of church leaders and to facilitate relationships between them. We started a local church network that began to meet once a term for breakfast. Many had never sat in the same room together, due to their significant differences in theology and praxis, but we began to build relationships. Early on I realised that so many issues divided the group, but there were two matters where they were united – a love for Jesus and a concern for the poor. So that is where we focused; building relationships, praying together and discussing ways to work together for the benefit of the community.

After several years of trust building we extended the geographical reach of the group to include the entire London borough of Merton. I can remember at one breakfast discussing how we could work more closely together and someone suggested changing our meeting frequency from every four months to every month. I was delighted when the group immediately agreed. Our commitment to build relationships and identify together has come a long way and there's still a way to go.

One of the things that I thought would add fresh energy to the group and really ground us in the needs of the local community, was a regular visit from our Member of Parliament, Police Commander and local authority chief executive who could talk about the challenges and opportunities they were facing. This was the only forum where local public figures could meet with all the church leaders in a single place, so it was easy to get them to attend. From the church leaders' perspective, I think they were partly curious and also rather flattered that they were being taken seriously by civic leaders.

The churches were increasingly keen to engage in activities that served the local community, so we would make a point of profiling potential new projects in our meetings. If it was a new community project that we wanted to start, we would co-ordinate which church would run it and encourage the cross-fertilisation of volunteers. The sharing of volunteers is a surprisingly sensitive issue for some pastors who fear that if a member gets involved in a project run by another church, they may shift their loyalty to that congregation. Together we worked through these issues, and various others, remembering always to keep our focus on those things that united us – loving God and loving our neighbour.

Merton316, as it became known, certainly hasn't solved church unity and partnership working, but it is a significant expression of church unity across the London borough of Merton.

In the summer of 2011 community riots erupted across a number of London boroughs. The churches responded, alongside many other community members, offering help to the police and local governments. The Church in London, however, had no capital-wide means of communication and co-ordination. I remember discussing this over lunch with a friend and wondering how many of London's thirty-two boroughs had a local church network like Merton316. So I started some relational research and discovered that twenty-eight of the thirty-two boroughs had a local church network. Some had been operating for a couple of decades, like the one in the London Borough of Newham, and others for a few months, like the London Borough of Ealing group.

I talked with the leaders of these local church networks about meeting together as a city-wide network for London and was delighted to be greeted by a resounding resonance. So at the start of 2012, the leaders of twenty-eight church networks met together in a venue provided by a senior officer in the Metropolitan Police. What began to emerge was what we called the London Network of Networks, a capital-wide network of borough-based networks. Yes, that's a lot of networks!
One of the greatest challenges in developing the London

Network of Networks was the triple pressure that church leaders felt. Leaders were naturally committed to their 'local parish' and by nature of the fact that I had identified them they were also committed to the local church network in their borough and now I was inviting them to become committed to a capital network. That's a lot of commitments to negotiate. But there was clearly an appetite for collaboration and, as is the characteristic pattern of these networks, food, relationship building and prayer ensued.

The Met Police provided venues for our meetings and so we began to develop a natural affiliation with them and subsequently support for them through prayer. The outcomes of the meetings often took us by surprise. Through a relationship I had with Met Police HR, I had been involved as an independent assessor on police promotion interview panels. I casually asked if this was an area where they could do with additional support – it turned out it was. At its peak twenty-five members of the London Network of Networks became involved as independent assessors helping choose the senior officers that would police our capital – all thanks to relationships that we had built with them.

In time, the Met Police appointed a Commander for Community Engagement who really understood and appreciated the difference local churches made in their communities. Together we hosted a joint meeting of London's thirty-two Borough Police Commanders and their corresponding London Network of Network borough leader. This really helped build stronger relationships between local churches and police forces.

But we need to remember that, whilst London is the largest city in the UK, it is just one area. Cities, towns and villages across the country face their own social and economic challenges. David King is a leader and man of prayer in Salford, Manchester. As a boy Dave remembers walking the Salford derelict docklands with his father praying for restoration of an area which had become abandoned and forgotten. Then in 2004 the BBC made the decision to move to Salford and so followed the development of Media City and the physical and commercial restoration of the area.

Dave visited the London Network of Networks and prayed with us for the restoration of the capital. During our time together Dave commented on the resentment that exists across much of the country towards London. With the seat of our Parliament and Government in London, decisions that are made can often feel London-centric despite high levels of representation. London is also our financial capital and there is a resentment toward the 'fat cat' salaries and bonuses that are paid in comparison to salaries across the rest of the country. Over time this has led to a general feeling that London has a rather arrogant attitude and a sense of entitlement to the privileges enjoyed there. In light of this, it was extremely moving to see Dave prophetically declare that for the UK to thrive, the country needs London to thrive. So as a 'Salford boy' he prayed on behalf of the rest of the UK for London to be blessed. He also walked across London's thirty-two boroughs stopping at each town hall to pray with church and civic leaders for the blessing and transformation of our capital.

The London Network of Networks has not arrived, we are on a journey towards greater unity in Jesus for the transformation of our capital city and country. There is much more for us to learn and do, but I'm pleased to say that we are on the journey.

Merton316 and the London Network of Networks illustrate what God is doing all over the UK and all over the world in starting local church networks. It is exciting to hear the stories of local church networks emerging in other cities and countries such as Together for Berlin (Germany), ACCL (Amsterdam, Netherlands), City Story (Durban, South Africa), OneChurch (Toowoomba, Australia), Church United (Fort Lauderdale, South Florida), City Serve (New York City) and City Serve Portland (Oregon).

Recently the London Network of Networks and Together for Berlin joined forces for a 'capital connection'. We have committed to each other in relationship, prayer and learning towards mutual city transformation. We stood together at the site of the historic Berlin Wall that annexed West Berlin from East Berlin between 1961–1989 and not only divided a nation but divided families and communities. We prayed for reconciliation and unity between our capitals and between all people.

What the capital connection will become, will emerge further as relationships grow. However, it gives me great excitement to think that there is now a new bridge between our two capitals.

Greater connections and greater communication, I believe, can only be a good thing. Wherever I travel in the world I meet church leaders who are feeling the tension between their commitment to their congregation and their city. If they invest in their congregation, some think they are not directly investing in their city and if they invest in their city some think they are not directly investing in their congregation. However, I don't believe the two are mutually exclusive.

One of the measures of success for any church leader is the size of their Sunday congregation – it's just one of those things we never seem to get past. The first question we can ask about someone's church is, "How big is it?" As a result, many church leaders become rather territorial and protective about their congregation. It can also make them feel nervous when a new church is planted. Even though these church leaders know that more churches are needed to reach the different sectors of the community, church members remain susceptible to the latest fad and that remains a challenge in our 'size-concerned' world.

Sometimes people bemoan the many church denominations and networks that exist – why are we not one Church? In reality we wouldn't want them to exist as one denomination because the diversity we see between our denominations expresses something of God's creativity. Our unity in the midst of our diversity is a greater testament to God's love and relationships than a monochromatic and generic version of ourselves with less space for diversity and freedom of expression. Unity and uniformity are very different – thankfully God has called us to one and not the other.

This diversity within the church is something that is clear throughout the Bible. The Bible is full of paradoxes; I like to lean into apparent contradictions because it is there that I find dynamic truth. We find one such paradox in the way the Bible talks about the unity of the Church. When Paul writes to the Church in the city of Ephesus, he is emphatic that there is one Church – fact – just as there is one Spirit, one hope, one Lord, one faith, one baptism and one God (Ephesians 4:3-6). However, in the Gospel of John, Jesus prays that the Church may be one just as he and the Father are one (John 17) expressing how the unity of the Church is something that we need to pray and work towards. This is the reality of the Kingdom of God on Earth as it is in heaven, that it is available now and that it is not fully complete.

Over forty years ago Pastor Ian Shelton, from a city called Toowoomba in eastern Australia, believed God told him to change the way he viewed the different denominations. Instead of seeing them as different churches he began seeing one Church but many congregations. This thinking has now directly and indirectly impacted many unity networks around the world. He began to gather church leaders to pray together and through this unity many initiatives to transform the city have emerged. More than forty years on, the reality of one Church with multiple congregations is still something that is being prayed and worked towards.

In the midst of wrestling for greater unity, we know that we are stronger together than we are apart. If we are one, people are more likely to believe us and our communities, cities and countries will be transformed.

How do we join in?

1. *What level of relational unity exists between the church leaders in your community, city and country?*

2. *How could you encourage a greater level of trust between churches?*

3. *How could you help prioritise Jesus and the poor over other secondary issues of faith that are currently a barrier between leaders?*

4. *What would it take for your local church to see itself as part of one Church in your locality?*

4

Prayer Rising

When I shut up the heavens so that there is no rain, or command locusts to devour the land or send a plague among my people, if my people, who are called by my name, will humble themselves and pray and seek my face and turn from their wicked ways, then I will hear from heaven, and I will forgive their sin and will heal their land.
(2 Chronicles 7:13-14)

What is God doing?

Every historic move of God has been preceded by intense prayer. God is stirring his Church around the world to pray in new ways, with new fervour and with new levels of mobilisation. Prayer in rising.

One Sunday morning my three children and I sat on the sofa and read the Bible together. We turned to the book of Jonah and my youngest son Reuben read about how God called Jonah to go to Nineveh and speak on his behalf. Then my daughter Matilda read how Jonah ran away and went to sea to try and escape God and how he ended up being swallowed by a large fish who spat him out three days later. Then Joseph, my eldest son, read about God calling Jonah for the second time to go to Nineveh and speak his message. Despite Nineveh being a Godless city, the people responded in fasting, repentance and prayer and, as a result, God relented and did not bring on the city the destruction he had planned. Consequently, Jonah was so cross with God that he ran away to the east of the city where he sulked.

When the children and I finished reading the book of Jonah I turned to Reuben, who was seven years old at the time, and asked, "Reuben, what did you think of Jonah?" He replied, "Daddy, Jonah had an anger management problem because whenever things didn't go his way he got cross". I then turned to Matilda, who was nine years old, and asked, "Matilda, what do you think of Jonah?" She replied, "Daddy, Jonah was a coward because whenever things didn't go his way he ran away". Finally, I turned to Joseph, who was 11 years old, and said, "Joseph, what do you think of Jonah?" He replied, "Daddy, Jonah was a drama queen because whenever anything went wrong he wanted to kill himself". We sat on the sofa and talked about Jonah's gremlins and how he wrestled with them in order to follow God's calling on his life.

Later I looked at Jonah again and asked myself the same question I had asked my children. What I learned from

Jonah was that if we can speak to civic leaders in a way they can understand it can invoke prayer and lead to the transformation of cities.

The Biblical paradigm aligns with historical experience that intense prayer precedes transformational moves of God. The challenge is to make prayer a central part of what is essentially a very secular society. The challenge is to work with community and civic leaders in ways that they can understand. If we can achieve this, then we can invoke prayer, fasting and repentance that results in transformation, which is why I have come to thank Jonah for teaching me 'the principle of city transformation.'

The Redeemed Christian Church of God (RCCG) is the largest black church denomination and one of the fastest growing church movements in the world. It is committed to intense prayer for revival and gathers very large numbers of people for all night prayer events around the world. For more than five years I have been helping with the Festival of Life, which is their UK prayer event hosted at the Excel Centre in East London and gathers more than 40,000 people who pray from 8pm to 5am.

A few years ago my friend Pastor Agu Irukwu, Senior Pastor of RCCG Jesus House in London, took me to the Holy Ghost prayer event in Lagos, Nigeria. I don't know about you, but until I attended this event I had never seen a crowd of more than a million people before. But that's the number of people that they gather together to pray. We drove around the crowd which went on and on for ever and ever – it was truly awe inspiring to see a million people gathered together to pray. The RCCG are investing in intense prayer all around the world.

The last time I spoke at the RCCG Festival of Life I launched Cinnamon Network's invitation to the Church to host Civic Prayer Events in villages, towns and cities around the UK and beyond. Civic Prayer Events are not new, the National Prayer Breakfast movement hosted in parliaments around the world started in the US in 1953 and has been attended by every US President at least once ever since. The National Prayer Breakfast family is an incredible movement of prayer within parliaments around the world. The focus is on the person of Jesus and gathering political leaders and other influential leaders around him. By focusing on Jesus, we remove human barriers of politics, religion or any other ideologies.

What is unique about Civic Prayer Events is that they are focused on local governments rather than national ones. Civic Prayer Event organisers are encouraged to visit key leaders involved in business, education, health, media, politics, policing and community (the cultural transformation framework which I will explain in Chapter 7) and ask them what their greatest needs are. It is then explained that a Civic Prayer Event is being hosted where these needs will be prayed for and would they like to attend. Whilst the focus is very much on Jesus-centred prayer, the whole event is held in a neutral civic venue and accessible to those of all faiths and none.

The Pentecostal in me believes that when we pray, God changes things and the Monastic in me believes that when we pray God changes us. When I turned forty years old I took a day retreat to pray and reflect. I asked a group of my friends what questions they thought I should be asking myself. And so I went away and sought God's guidance.

I have to say, I was quite surprised with what God revealed in my heart. As an 'A-Type driven leader', I like to be busy, to get things done and I'm generally not afraid to stick my neck out. However, I realised my greatest ambition was to be a man of peace. Needless to say this came as quite a surprise to those around me. What was clear to me was that I was not going to become a man of peace by simply continuing as I was before; something needed to change. I needed to find a new dimension and depth to my life of prayer. As I pursued this thought, I came across the monastic tradition where the emphasis of prayer is putting ourselves in a place where God can transform us.

Moses discovered that prayer enabled God to both change things and change him. For example, when Israel started to regret their decision to leave Egypt because they were hungry and thirsty, Moses prayed to God who made provision for them (Genesis 16). When Moses returned from praying to God on Mount Sinai he was changed; his face was radiant because he had spent time with God (Exodus 34:29). My hope and expectation through the Civic Prayer Events is that God will change communities and the churches within them.

The Times newspaper recently reported on the Civic Prayer Events with the headline, 'Civic leaders start praying to renew our towns and cities' and explained that, 'In some cases the prayer events will mark the start of formal agreements in which local churches are placed at the heart of a town or city's civic life… Conscious that it is the sort of idea that could be spectacularly counter-productive if done insensitively, the Cinnamon Network had drawn up a list of prescriptions. Top of the list is not to hold the event in a church, but ideally in the town hall so that the civic life of the town or city is the focus'. It is hoped that renewed prayer will lead to greater engagement between the church, community and civic organisations leading to transformation.

Placing prayer at the centre of city-life has had a dramatic impact in other cities across the world. Recently I had the privilege of meeting a businessman from Cape Town, South Africa called Graham Power who in 2000 had a dream that God was asking him to host a prayer event for the needs of South Africa. In 2001 he hosted a prayer gathering and 45,000 Christians filled the Newlands Stadium in Cape Town. This became a global movement of prayer. On Pentecost Sunday in 2010 a Global Day of Prayer united every nation on earth mobilising 400 million people to pray.

24/7 Prayer is another incredible global prayer movement that started in a warehouse on an industrial estate on the south coast of England in 1999. It all began with Roger Ellis, Pete Greig and a group in their church who believed that prayer should be at the heart of their Christian life, but who also recognised that they were pretty bad at it. In response, they took the rather drastic step of opening up a room in a warehouse to pray 24 hours a day, seven days a week. Now, nearly two decades on, 10,000 prayer rooms have been hosted in more than half the nations on earth and more than two million people have taken part.

In recent years there has also been an increase in the number of 'houses of prayer'. In the UK alone there are now around thirty-five and many more around the world. Their common vision is to establish a non-denominational prayer and worship hub focused on activating prayer for transformation in specific communities and cities. In 2001 William and Karen Porter in Stoke-on-Trent sensed God's call, "I want you to build me a house of radical worship, teaching and prayer, where the lost will be saved, the sick healed, the downtrodden raised up and my glory revealed. It shall be a holy house, a light on a hill, marked by my presence which you will carry to the nations". In the years that followed they have opened The Beacon as a house of prayer for the city and the nations. Stories of God calling people to open houses of prayer are happening around the world.

These are just a handful of the hundreds of stories to show the growing momentum and intensity of prayer around the world. This suggests that we are on the cusp of a global move of God – please!

How do we join in?

1. *What do you believe happens when you pray?*

2. *How could you encourage greater prayer for the transformation of your community, city or country?*

3. *What would it take to host a Civic Prayer Event to benefit your community?*

4. *Where have you seen intense prayer for your country grow over recent years and how could you fuel that further?*

5

A Force for Good

What good is it, my brothers and sisters, if someone claims to have faith but has no deeds? Can such faith save them? Suppose a brother or a sister is without clothes and daily food. If one of you says to them, "Go in peace; keep warm and well fed," but does nothing about their physical needs, what good is it? In the same way, faith by itself, if it is not accompanied by action, is dead.
(James 2:14-17)

What is God doing?

Over the last two decades the attitude of the Church to social action and community engagement has changed dramatically. Social action used to be seen as the preserve of the liberal and catholic wing of the Church. However, much of the evangelical, pentecostal and broad church is now leading the way on social engagement. I believe that God is mainstreaming social action and community engagement across the full breadth of the Church and positioning churches at the heart of communities, cities and countries as a force for good.

Queen Elizabeth II in her 2016 Christmas message to the British people said, "We can sometimes think the world's problems are so big that we can do little to help. On our own we cannot end wars or wipe out injustice but, the cumulative impact of thousands of small acts of goodness can be bigger than we imagine." She then went on to talk about how Jesus inspired her in her own faith. Sometimes we use the excuse that we can't systemically end social problems as a reason to do nothing at all. However, our small contribution alongside everyone else's makes a very significant difference indeed, so there are no excuses for abdicating responsibility.

Cinnamon Network began when we saw what we thought was a divine pattern for addressing local social need on a significant national scale. Across the UK we saw innovative local church community projects springing up. When other churches saw how impacting these projects were, they went to investigate and immediately saw that they too could replicate the projects in their churches and communities. And so we found that across the country there were the beginnings of the natural of replication effective social action projects. The beauty was that churches were sharing ideas and models, rather than spending time and money reinventing the wheel, as it were. So Cinnamon

Network started a partnership between these projects to join in and accelerate the process of replication.

Cinnamon now has a menu of brilliant community projects that can be easily replicated by local churches. The portfolio began with just a handful of replicable community projects including Street Pastors, which helps churches address anti-social behaviour, Food Banks, which helps churches provide relief for those caught in food poverty and CAP, which helps churches get people out of debt. Since then, Cinnamon has developed expertise at identifying and supporting the growth of new replicable local church community projects.

Every great social action project has to start somewhere, so we have made a point of seeking out great new projects and helping them to grow, through the Cinnamon Incubator, to a point where they can be replicated across the country. Make Lunch was one of the first projects Cinnamon incubated. The founder Rachel Warwick became aware that 1.4 million children who receive free school dinners during term time, because their parent or parents were assessed to be too poor to provide them with a packed lunch or money for a school meal, often went hungry during the holidays. She responded by phoning three friends in three local churches and during that first summer they made lunch for children who would otherwise go hungry. Now Make Lunch help local churches all over the UK develop a relationship with a local school or schools to invite children to enjoy a healthy meal during the school holidays. Within two years, fift-six local churches ran Make Lunch and made 11,500 meals for children who would otherwise have gone hungry.

Welcome Box is another powerful example. When the European refugee crisis/opportunity reached its peak during the summer of 2015 Cinnamon reached out to a local church in Derby who had been running an impactful project to welcome and resettle refugees. The church had built a relationship of trust with the local council so whenever refugees were rehoused in the city the local church received a referral. Two trained volunteers would then visit the refugee in their new home to offer a warm welcome alongside practical support. The volunteers would also take a box of token welcome gifts for the family together along with local information to help them settle in. The volunteers were often the first members of the community that many refugees would meet. During the first year of incubation, Welcome Box was replicated by groups of local churches in twenty-five towns and cities.

Care Home Friends is an even more recent project. In the UK 1 million elderly people live alone, 500,000 of them spend Christmas day on their own every year. Research has shown that if they live in a care home, they are twice as likely to feel lonely as they are in the community. So Care Home Friends was established to help local churches build a relationship with a local care home for the elderly and adopt them by offering a visiting and befriending service. In particular, volunteers are trained in caring for those with dementia, Alzheimer's and other issues related to that stage of life.

We are aware that many more churches across the country are doing amazing things to support those in need within their community. Often these churches are just getting on with loving God and loving their neighbour, but if other churches knew about these projects, they too could replicate them and start impacting their own communities. In order to extend the range of Cinnamon Recognised Projects, each year Cinnamon runs a campaign to find the best of what local churches are doing to transform their communities and develop those projects to a point where they can be replicated by other churches.

Hundreds of thousands of people engage with the campaign and, after rounds of applications and shortlisting, five local church community projects are invited to present their initiative in a 'Dragons' Den' or 'Shark Tank' style event. The winning projects are awarded a place on the Cinnamon Incubator where they receive two years of training and financial support to develop their project to a point where it can be replicated in multiple churches.

Cinnamon UK offers a menu of more than thirty local church community projects that are recognised as excellent and which can easily be put into practice by others. Cinnamon International is now looking to work with the Church in other countries to help them develop their own menu of community projects that can be easily replicated by local churches. This will increase the speed and effectiveness of their community transformation work by saving them from needlessly reinventing the wheel.

Of course, we are aware that many of the issues that we are addressing are deep-rooted. Being the 'Good Samaritan' (Luke 10) who stops to help the man who has been robbed is good but it is not enough. We also need to deal with the root causes of the problem and fix the 'Jericho Road' that the man was robbed on in the first place. Sometimes dealing with the root causes of a problem requires an educational solution so that people know how to travel on the road safely, which might mean during daylight hours or in groups. Dealing with the root cause may also mean seeing justice is done and imprisoning the robbers so that they can go through a rehabilitation process. It might also mean lobbying the local authority to have street lights improved, CCTV fitted or the road built in such a way as there are no places for robbers to hide. Equally, it may also mean engaging with the robbers themselves to find out what drives them so that those issues can be addressed.

Cinnamon community projects help meet both the immediate presenting need and the root causes of the problem. For example, Food Banks are a very practical way of providing immediate relief to people caught in food poverty – however, they don't solve anything longer term. The root cause of food poverty may be long term unemployment or crippling debt, so job clubs that help local churches get people back into work and money advice that helps people restructure their debts and pay them off are also essential.

The replication of local church community projects is happening all over the world. In Ethiopia, Kale Heywet Church started a self-help group to help 15-20 people to save very small amounts of money each week. At the same time, they learnt basic skills such as book keeping and managing finances. After a few months the group began making loans to each other to help start small businesses. Over time their livelihoods were transformed as the self-help group became a powerful network of encouragement and support. Fifteen years later there are now around 14,000 self-help groups across Ethiopia, all helping individuals to manage their finances and escape from debt and poverty.

In this context the question I hear most frequently asked by church leaders is, "We would like to do something more in the community, but we are just not sure what?" Umoja, which is Swahili for 'togetherness' is a way of helping local churches to work together to pool their resources in order to support their community in addressing social needs. It was pioneered by churches in Uganda, replicated through churches across the developing world. The Cinnamon Network team of Church and Community Advisors are helping churches on a very similar pathway of asking what are the priority needs of the community, what are the resources God has given us as a congregation and what best practice project best brings those needs and resources together.

Churches are becoming more aware of the acute social need and developing responses more quickly. Northern Ireland and the Republic of Ireland have high levels of mental health issues and suicide, Germany and Greece are receiving large numbers of refugees and England and others are confronted with increasing domestic violence. South Africa is plagued by educational and economic injustice, France is facing increasing levels of radicalisation and terrorism and Eastern European countries are wrestling with high levels of youth unemployment. These are pressing social issues that local churches are increasingly responding to. In doing so, they are repositioning themselves at the heart of every community, city and country as powerful agents for transformation. Followers of Jesus are becoming a force for good in society.

How do we join in?

1. *What are the most pressing social needs within your local community?*

2. *What are the passions and resources God has given your church?*

3. *Could it help to speak with a Cinnamon Network Church and Community Advisor about developing a way forward?*

4. *What is your motivation for helping people in need? Are you selfless or do you have an ulterior motive?*

5. *What are the most pressing social needs in your country and what could you and others do about them?*

6. *Are you involved in a local church community project that is changing lives and that, if replicated, could help other local churches change lives?*

7. *What would it take for your church to be known as a force for good?*

6

Cultural Change

> *For the creation was subjected to frustration, not by its own choice, but by the will of the one who subjected it, in hope that the creation itself will be liberated from its bondage to decay and brought into the freedom and glory of the children of God. We know that the whole creation has been groaning as in the pains of childbirth right up to the present time.*
> (Romans 8:20-22)

What is God doing?

For many years the Church has embraced a sacred secular divide that has led people in the marketplace to feel like their main contribution is to give money to their church, bring guests to their services and sit quietly and listen to their church leader. God is awakening people to see their marketplace as their sacred calling and the primary context in which to pursue kingdom transformation.

God provides those who follow him with three mandates. The first is the creation mandate, it is to "Be fruitful and increase in number: fill the earth and subdue it," in other words – to lead creation (Genesis 1:28). This is why the late Myles Munroe, a highly respected Christian leader, said, "We are born to lead" because that is God's creation mandate for humanity. The second mandate we were given is the great commandment, which is to love God and love our neighbour as we love our self (Matthew 22:37-39), which as we know is a lot harder than it sounds. Finally, the third mandate is the great commission which is about making disciples of all nations (Matthew 28:19).

The Church tradition we come from will often influence which of the three mandates we place greatest emphasis on. The creation mandate is primarily about cultural change which is what this chapter is about. The great commandment is about social action, which is what the last chapter was about, and the great commission is all about evangelism and discipleship which we'll explore in the next chapter. However, it's important to remember that whatever our church tradition, we are actually mandated to do all three.

One of the things that I love about travelling internationally is the space it can provide to think and pray. Whilst on a trip to Ghana I asked myself, "What is my vision for the Church and society?" As soon as I'd asked it, I realised what I should have been asking was, "What is God's vision for the Church and society?" I picked up my Bible and read…

> *The Son is the image of the invisible God, the firstborn over all creation. For in him all things were created: things in heaven and on earth, visible and invisible, whether thrones or powers or rulers or authorities; all things have been created through him and for him. He is before all things, and in him all things hold together. And he is the head of the body, the church; he is the beginning and the firstborn from among the dead, so that in everything he might have the supremacy. For God was pleased to have all his fullness dwell in him, and through him to reconcile to himself all things, whether things on earth or things in heaven, by making peace through his blood, shed on the cross.*
>
> (Colossians 1:15-20).

God is a God of 'all things' not 'some things'. He created all things, he sustains all things and he reconciles all things. There is no sacred and secular divide, whereby some jobs and activities are sacred and other jobs and activities are secular. The only thing that is secular, or without God, is sin so let's call it sin not something else. So if a job or activity isn't sinful it can be sacred, as the Apostle Paul said, whatever you work at, work at it with all your heart as if for God and not for men. I have always believed that if a person cannot find God in their work they should find new work. Work consumes so much of our waking life that it is an awful waste to do something you don't find God in.

So what are the 'all things' of God's creation? In 1975 a couple of American Christian leaders called Bill

Bright and Lauren Cunningham believed that God had given them a vision to bring Godly influence to 'Seven Mountains of Culture'. The seven mountains as they saw them were: arts and entertainment, business, education, family, government, media and religion. Until now this model has helpfully influenced the Churches to think about and practice cultural transformation.

I believe there are a number of aspects of this cultural transformation framework that can now be improved and updated. Firstly, I have called the 'mountains' sectors because that's what the people outside the Church who we want to work with would call them. Secondly, I have removed 'religion' because I believe that Jesus Christ is present in all the sectors and I wanted to avoid a sacred secular mindset and approach. Thirdly, I merged 'media' with 'arts and entertainment' because there has been a convergence of those sectors over the past few decades. Fourthly, I've added an additional sector 'health and well-being'. I think it's interesting that the initial cultural transformation model was conceived within an American mindset which has struggled around the issue to healthcare provision. Fifthly, I've added 'policing and security', given the growing threats to the safety of our communities and nations. So this creates a cultural transformation framework that has seven sectors:

1. Business and Finance
2. Education and Learning

3. Health and Wellbeing
4. Media, Arts and Entertainment
5. Politics and Government
6. Policing and Security
7. Family and Community

Once you have an understanding of what the 'all things' that God has originated, sustains and reconciles are, you can do all sorts of things with them. I was involved with the leadership of a local church where each week we would interview someone in the church community who embodied Christ in one of the sectors. We were careful that these talks were about how they fulfilled their role in a transformational way that realised the Kingdom of God rather than a transactional way that was only trying to convert people.

My wife Esther was interviewed at our church about her work as a special education needs coordinator at our local primary school. She told stories of children who struggled with education and for whom she secured statutory provision to support them in their education – this is truly life changing. She talked about how parents ask her for help with a whole range of needs, such as completing forms to obtain additional funding from the local government. She talked about telephoning the mum of a child after his first week at the school, the mum immediately thought the child was in trouble and then Esther explained that she was telephoning to say how well the child had done in their first week. The parent had never been contacted by a teacher to say something positive about their child – she was overwhelmed. These are stories of transformation.

Transformation is possible anywhere and one of the most exciting businesses that I have come across in recent years is Giant Worldwide, a global leadership and cultural change consultancy based in the United States. They have one of the strongest, most positive and most liberating organisational cultures that I have ever experienced. Having met their clients, I am left in no doubt that they really do transform people, teams and organisations. One of their values is 'to fight for the highest possible good in others' and I saw this expressed at the closing dinner of a conference where people spoke out short affirmations about other people in the room. It was electrifying to witness colleagues call out the good that they saw in other people.

Paul Szkiler runs an organisation called A Call To Business, which started work in Sierra Leone in 2006. At that time UN sanctions and roadblocks were in place, following the eleven-year conflict that tore the country apart at almost every level. The capital, Freetown was thrown into darkness every night, with no power to generate lighting. To top things off, it was vying with Malawi for the dubious distinction of being the poorest nation on the globe. Great strides have taken place since that time with successive, democratically elected governments moving the country forward. A Call To Business is now the second largest micro-finance provider in Sierra Leone, with more than 8,000 clients receiving loans to start businesses, some of which have developed into SMEs (Small to Medium Enterprises). What an incredible transformational impact.

Cultural transformation requires leaders who can cross between sectors with ease. At this time, austerity is driving greater cross sector relationships and partnerships because no one organisation or sector has all the resources required to achieve its objectives. In addition, the lines and relationships between for profit, not for profit and public sectors are becoming increasingly blurred. Not for profits are pursuing social enterprise, profits are becoming more socially responsible and the public sector is becoming privatised and seeking more partnership opportunities with the voluntary community sector.

As they negotiate so many different sectors, our leaders have a natural or developed cultural dexterity and agility. They swiftly gain an appreciation of an environment, build relationships and feel at 'home'. They are culturally nimble, supple and flexible so that in a short time they can relate and interact in any culture or sector. By contrast, people, buildings or ideologies that lack dexterity and agility are brittle and when faced with significant stress can break.

The author and business scholar, Judi Neal, calls these leaders Edgewalkers in her book of the same name. She explains that, "The organisations that will thrive in the 21st century are organisations that embrace and nurture Edgewalkers. These unusual leaders have learned to walk in many different worlds without getting completely caught up in any of them. They are bridge builders who link different paradigms, cultural boundaries, and worldviews." One of the ways you become an Edgewalker is simply to spend time with people, build relationships, attend events and participate in programmes outside your normal sector and, often, outside your comfort zone. You will learn by absorption and osmosis about the language used in these sectors, ways of working, stakeholder relationships and evaluation metrics. It is this cultural dexterity and agility that is critical in enabling leaders to cross the boundaries of different sectors and cultures.

Workplaces in the UK are becoming increasingly diverse. This is partly the result of government legislation and also a growing awareness that diversity can bring freshness to innovation, problem solving, productivity and profitability. This has led to many corporate businesses setting up diversity networks to increase the engagement, motivation and retention of minority people groups. Among these are women's networks, African networks and faith networks – including Christian networks. This provides an incredible opportunity for followers of Jesus to meet on the businesses premises with official recognition and sometimes with a company's budget for catering, speakers and other activities. Their mandate is to add value to the business by encouraging people to bring their whole selves to work – what an opportunity to transform culture!

One of the ways I use this cultural transformation framework is in my personal prayers. As there are seven sectors and seven days of the week, I pray for a different sector and the leaders, institutions and friends I know within that sector each day. I use the days of the week to help guide my prayers. Monday is the start of the working week so I pray for business and finance. Tuesday I think about my children going to school and so pray for education and learning. Wednesday I pray for health and well-being. Thursday I have the tradition of going to a jazz club, which reminds me to pray for media, arts and entertainment. On Friday Members of Parliament are in their constituencies which reminds me to pray for politics and government. Saturday I think about football matches which reminds me to pray for police and security. Sunday is a family day so I pray for other families and community.

This focus on workplace leadership is one that can sometimes be relegated to a brief mention within the liturgy of our Sunday services. However, the vast majority of Biblical characters and leaders were not priests or religious professionals, they were parents and children, people working in business, politics, finance, welfare and agriculture, as well as neighbours and civic leaders. One of the things I would like to do one day is a seven-part speaking series focused on these seven sectors of society. I would base each talk on a Biblical character who worked in that sector and tell the stories of people who are working in those sectors in transformational ways today. Business and finance could be Lydia (Acts

16), education and learning could be Ezra (Ezra 7), health and well-being could be Doctor Luke (Luke & Acts), media, arts and entertainment could be King David (1 Samuel and Psalms), politics and government could be Joseph (Genesis 37-50), policing and security could be Deborah (Judges 6) and family and community Nehemiah (Nehemiah).

I've known some larger churches that have set up support and discipleship networks that gather together people from specific sectors for support and prayer. Others have run prayer events focused on supporting people working in different sectors. There isn't always the capacity to do this in small churches, but there is definitely scope to develop these networks throughout towns and cities as unity and trust grows between local churches.

The Bible is clear that the role of local church leaders is not to do all the works of service themselves, but 'to equip his people for works of service' (Ephesians 4:12), whether that be in their home, community, not for profit, for profit or public sector organisations. I know some church leaders who make a point of visiting and praying for people in their workplaces, others who deliberately take a part-time marketplace role in order to keep themselves connected and some who take it upon themselves to make contact on a regular basis with leaders of different sectors of society.

The whole of creation, communities, cities, countries and the varying marketplaces within them are groaning with the pains of new birth as it is reconciled to God through Jesus Christ. As the whole body of Christ recognises its sacred calling in the marketplace, then it will play an even more instrumental role in restoration and transformation.

How do we join in?

1. *How do you see, and could you increasingly see, your work as a sacred calling and an act of worship?*

2. *If you genuinely can't find God in your work, how do you feel about the possibility of finding new work?*

3. *How could you influence your local church to place a greater emphasis on recognising, valuing and supporting people in the marketplace?*

4. *Could you think about starting a group, big or small, for people working in the same or in a similar sector?*

7

Talking Jesus

All authority in heaven and on earth has been given to me. Therefore go and make disciples of all nations, baptising them in the name of the Father and the Son and of the Holy Spirit, and teaching them to obey everything I have commanded you. And surely I am with you always, to the very end of the age.
(Matthew 28:18-20)

What is God doing?

It may be our British reserve, but we seem to have lived through a number of decades, even the long-forgotten and so-called 'decade of evangelism', when talking about Jesus in public has become ever so slightly embarrassing. This season is changing. In the UK, the wave of change is, in no small part, thanks to the Archbishop of Canterbury, Justin Welby. Justin talks openly, normally and disarmingly about Jesus Christ and in doing so he has won the confidence of the British media who, in the past have taken a less than favourable approach to reporting what church leaders have to say.

On 30th November 2016 the British Prime Minster Theresa May made a statement in Parliament supporting a report saying that Christians should "jealously guard their right to speak about their faith at work and in public places". Not every Prime Minister, government and nation welcomes talking about Jesus in the public square in this way. It's definitely true that not every country enjoys the freedom of religion or encourages the expression of faith in public life like the UK does.

The religious freedom charity, Christian Solidarity Worldwide, explain that, "Three quarters of the world's population lives in countries with severe restrictions on their religious freedom – in fact, it's one of the most widely-violated human rights in the world." It is too easy for those of us who live in nations where there is religious freedom to take our ability to talk so freely about Jesus for granted.

At this time, God is increasing the confidence and courage of the UK Church to 'talk Jesus' as he is in a number of other nations around the world. This chapter is named after the research project, 'Talking Jesus' conducted by Barna Group on behalf of the Church of England in collaboration with Hope Together and Evangelical Alliance. As you would expect, relationships are critically important in talking about Jesus. The research shows that, 'Most non-Christians (67%) in

England know a practising Christian – and that person is most likely to be a friend (40%) or family member (34%). For 15% of non-Christians, the Christian they know is an acquaintance, for 7% a colleague and for 4%, a neighbour. And they don't just know us; they like us too, with non-Christians more likely to describe us positively than negatively.' However, the research outlined one key challenge, 'More than half of non-Christians (54%) who know a Christian, have not had a conversation with this person about faith in Jesus.' So lots of people know a Christian but Christians are not talking about Jesus as much as they could.

A leader I met recently said, "We need to stop 'evangelising' because we are putting people off, instead we need to show people God's love and kindness and look for natural opportunities to talk Jesus". I'm not sure I agree, but I do understand the sentiment of what he is saying. If 'evangelism' is done to people in a way that is unhelpful or uninvited it can do more harm than good. We cannot talk or persuade people into becoming followers of Jesus. In reality, we witness to Jesus and then it's the Holy Spirit who changes people's hearts and minds. Fundamentally, conversion is a work of God not a work of people.

Laurence Singlehurst, author of best-selling book *Sowing, Reaping, Keeping: People-Sensitive Evangelism* said, "When talking about Jesus the rule of conversational tennis means that as long as people ask questions then you respond. However, when people stop asking questions you shut up, which means they never feel pressurised and leaves them open to the next Holy Spirit encounter." As mentioned in my early years of following Jesus I would try and push and persuade people to follow Jesus, but for all my trying I never managed to argue a single person into the Kingdom of God. Of course we are called to witness to Jesus, but ultimately our conversations will never convert people – only God can change people's hearts and minds.

What we need to remember is that good communication is focused on the customer rather than the seller, on the students rather than the teacher, on the unchurched rather than the churched. The audience determines the language, the tone, the style and the pace. It is the same when we talk Jesus – our communication should be determined by the hearer rather than the speaker.

One of the most incredible gifts that has helped local churches 'talk Jesus' is the Alpha Course, a ten-week series exploring Christianity, that was developed by Holy Trinity Brompton in London. It has helped the Church to provide an invitational context where people with varying different experiences of Church can come and hear about Jesus. It has also helped the Church be conversational about faith and provide an open, non-judgmental environment where people are encouraged to ask questions without fear of being disagreed with by an obnoxious Bible-quoting Christian who believes others must agree with them. Most of all, it has given the Church a real boost of confidence in the way it talks about faith.

We are called to influence (the creation mandate), to love (the great commandment) and tell (the great commission). There are times when I have heard leaders say that we have become too good at loving and not good enough at telling and that the pendulum needs to swing back the other way. The language of a "pendulum swinging" between loving and telling is harmful because it gives the impression that we might need to choose one or the other. We should not have to choose between showing people God and telling people about God. We don't improve at loving, by becoming worse at telling or vice versa. Instead, we should draw inspiration from what we are good at to fuel our all-round faith development.

The great commission always captivates with the overarching thought that our task is to disciple, or to make Jesus followers, out of nations. In the original language "nations" means people groups, so a nation as we know it can have many people groups within it. The Western world so easily defaults into thinking about discipling individuals, but Jesus' Eastern-mindset saw discipling and influencing in terms of whole communities, cities and nations. This more collective, holistic mindset is one that we in the Western world would benefit from. The Bible seamlessly integrates social action, cultural transformation and talking Jesus.

Some have, unfortunately, interpreted the great commission as the great escape. There are those who think that accepting and believing a certain set of beliefs is merely a way to endure this sinful and temporary earthly life. They live in a bubble of righteousness to prevent contamination from the world until they reach heaven.

The reality is that living for Jesus Christ means that we are partners in God's work of restoring the whole of creation right here and now, so it resembles that which he made it to be. Rather than being taken to heaven when Jesus comes again the Biblical direction of travel of God's purpose is from heaven to earth. The 'Holy City, new Jerusalem, coming down out of heaven from God' (Revelation 21:2) and "your kingdom come, your will be done, on earth as in heaven" (Matthew 6:10).

The World Migration Report 2015 explains that more than 54% of people across the globe were living in urban areas in 2014 and that the number of people living in cities will almost double to some 6.4 billion by 2050, turning much of the world into a global city. The renowned author, Tim Keller from Redeemer Church, New York made an interesting comment on our gospel responsibility in the face of mass urbanisation and the fact that three million people a week are moving to cities. "The world is moving to cities and if the Church is not strong in cities we will lose the world." Urbanisation is a massive challenge for the Church in talking Jesus, but we still have a missional challenge in rural communities. It's out here 'in the sticks' that we don't find idyllic chocolate box villages, but rather some of the greatest social and spiritual challenges for the gospel.

I was inspired recently to meet a young lady who runs a not for profit organisation. She finds people who have overcome a major challenge in their life and then works with them as a coach to help them share their story. She then invites groups of people to come together and hear a collection of these real life stories for themselves. After the event she gathers the speakers and celebrates them and offers them the opportunity to publish their stories as an inspiration to others. It was a real reminder to me that each one of us has our own incredible story of encountering Jesus. Wouldn't it be amazing if we shared these stories more often?

The strategy business McKinsey & Company in their report 'Using Stories to Lead Change' wrote, 'Human beings have been communicating with each other through storytelling and narrative since we lived in caves and sat around campfires. We might say storytelling is virtually hardwired into our DNA, we use stories to define ourselves, to make meaning and sense of the world, to teach values and pieces of wisdom, to engage others in change. We learn things at deep levels through hearing stories; they move us before we know why we are being moved; they affect us before we have time to put our defences up.' Story is very powerful and perhaps we should use it more to talk Jesus.

Let's pray for the continued growth of the Church's confidence and courage around the world when it comes to talking Jesus in their communities, cities and countries.

How do we join in?

1. *How could you positively influence your country's view of talking about faith in public life?*

2. *What percentage of your friends, colleagues and neighbours know you are a follower of Jesus?*

3. *From the way you live your life what do you think people who know you would say it means to be a follower of Jesus?*

4. *What are the opportunities you or your church could create for people to tell their Jesus story?*

5. *How can you help secure greater religious freedom in every nation?*

8

Good Community

God saw all that he had made, and it was very good
(Genesis 1: 31)

What is God doing?

For all the years I can remember, the Church has been talking about making a difference, transformation and revival. I have heard very little about what a healthy community looks like, but plenty about what full and healthy churches look like. It is true that the church models something to community about what it means to live together. However, that has sometimes been used as an excuse to say we are not ready yet. God is stirring his Church to imagine what transformed communities, cities and countries look like.

Whilst God was creating the world at each stage he said it was, "good" and when he had finished he stood back and said, "it was very good". He was not looking at the

Church he was looking at creation. Creation was good and pleasing to God. The big question is: what did God see in creation that made it so very good? What followed was the spoiling of God's creation (the fall) when it no longer looked so good. Since then God's mission has been to restore the whole of creation to the goodness that he originally made it to be (redemption).

Recently, I met with a group of church leaders to talk about community transformation. One of the pastors asked if good community would result in more people becoming Christians and bigger churches. I think he was hoping I was going to say yes but I didn't. Good community won't necessarily lead to more Christians and bigger churches – although it could well be a by product. Some people are caught in a way of thinking that highly values personal transformation but struggles to understand that the corporate transformation of community, city and country is just as much a part of God's plan.

Jesus came to earth living, breathing and demonstrating the Kingdom of God. The Bible records Jesus talking about the 'Church' just twice but he talked about the 'Kingdom of God' eighty-three times. The Kingdom of God is a dynamic alternative culture that provides a different way of seeing power and authority, of living and behaving, of thinking and feeling, of giving and receiving. The Kingdom of God, or Jesus culture, epitomises what good looks like and is in the process of restoring creation to what God intended it to be.

The human instinct is to despise those who despise you, to fight with those who fight you and to hate those who hate you. Jesus introduced an alternative approach, he said, "You have heard that it was said, 'Love your neighbour and hate your enemy.' But I tell you, love your enemies and pray for those who persecute you." (Matthew 5:34-35). What could be more radical than to fight hate with love. It reminds me of Martin Luther King Jr who in the African American civil rights movement advanced the approach of non-violent civil disobedience. During the campaign African American's were beaten and violated but King Jr maintained that hands should not be lifted in retaliation. It seemed crazy to not respond to violence with violence, but ultimately non-violence won.

Recently I visited Robben Island in South Africa where Nelson Mandela was incarcerated as a political prisoner for eighteen years. Our tour guide was a former political prisoner and so the stories that he told were first hand experiences. He invited us to ask him any question we liked and he would try and answer no matter how difficult it might be. So I asked, "Do you still feel angry about what happened to you and if not why not?" He talked about the anger he once had and how he had to fight within himself to overcome that and that now he felt no anger. He explained that, "Holding onto any negativity about someone else is like drinking poison and hoping they will be harmed by it". Hearing of such love even for enemies is humbling.

The Bible is full of paradoxes that completely throw into question the very truths we build our lives on. The beatitudes are a great example of Jesus putting forward a completely counter intuitive way of behaving that completely inverts what is accepted as normal. Jesus said, "Blessed are the poor in spirit, for theirs is the kingdom of heaven. Blessed are those who mourn, for they will be comforted. Blessed are the meek, for they will inherit the earth. Blessed are those who hunger and thirst for righteousness, for they will be filled. Blessed are the merciful, for they will be shown mercy. Blessed are the pure in heart, for they will see God. Blessed are the peacemakers, for they will be called children of God. Blessed are those who are persecuted because of righteousness, for theirs is the kingdom of heaven." (Matthew 5:3-11). Jesus made it clear he was for those who are down trodden, who are at their wits end, who are running on empty – this is his culture and his way and it was good.

The Kingdom of God turns things upside down or, perhaps it should be, right side up; it transforms bad into good, sadness into hope and poverty into wealth. As Jesus' manifesto declares, "The Spirit of the Lord is on me, because he has anointed me to proclaim good news to the poor. He has sent me to proclaim recovery of sight for the blind, to set the oppressed free, to proclaim the year of the Lord's favour" Luke (4:18-19). The Kingdom of God is a new world order in which creation is restored to good – which is what God intended it to be.

Jesus said, "I have come that they may have life, and have it to the full" (John 10:10). There would be some that would say Jesus' promise was for his followers only, but everything about his life and vocation was wildly inclusive and indicates that his promise was for all. So what does fullness of life look like for every member of your community and citizen of your city and country?

It's important to note there will always be a tension between good community and not so good community. Jesus also said, "The thief comes only to steal and to kill and to destroy" (John 10:10). We live in an epoch of time where the Kingdom of God is in the process of being realised on earth as it is in heaven. The Kingdom of God is both a now, and a not yet. A powerful example of this is when we pray for those who are sick; sometimes they are healed and sometimes they are not. This is the tension we live in, between the now and the not yet of the Kingdom of God. In heaven we know there will be no more sickness, but for now it's part of life.

There is a need for much more thinking to be done about what good looks like in our communities, cities and countries. We particularly need to know what good looks like in the seven sectors of society which I talked about earlier, namely: business and finance, education and learning, health and well-being, media, arts and entertainment, politics and government, policing and security and family and community. Once we have a clearer picture and target of what we want to see things transformed into, I believe we will begin to make more progress.

That work needs to be led and contextualised by those who inhabit and influence those sectors rather than by theologians or church leaders who play an important supporting role. God himself stepped into a specific context with a specific language, time and traditions. The Message translates the incarnation as 'the word became flesh and blood and moved into the neighbourhood' (John 1:14). Only when we live in a particular culture do we have the genuine ability and credibility to speak to it.

Jesus has never and will never exist outside of culture, he is always a contextual expression. The Church naturally contextualises Jesus to look like itself but, in doing so, there is the danger that one particular picture of Jesus becomes the absolute version. Walk into many churches and you'll still find pictures on the wall of a Caucasian Christ. This flies in the face of the most well-known fact about Christ, which is that he was born in Bethlehem, in the Middle East, so he would definitely not have been white. We all contextualise what we read about Jesus so it makes most sense to us. Church leaders are no different. They read the Bible through the lens of church leadership and often see every leader in the Bible as a religious professional, rather than the vast majority who were in fact politicians, soldiers, farmers, fisherman and vineyard owners. Context is critically important in understanding what good community looks like.

The Cinnamon Network leadership team have given a little time to considering what good community looks like and developed seven dimensions that it thinks are important. The first being responsible leadership, then a community vision and strategic plan, a thriving economy that is generative for the whole community, affirmation of strong families and households, the holistic development and well-being of every individual, affordable housing and community confidence, pride and resilience. Clearly these dimensions are discussion starters rather than established pillars of truth. If they are explored they will begin to provide a picture of what good community looks like.

To love a community, city or country well means enabling it to become all that God intended it to be – namely good! God is leading people to a greater sense of collective responsibility and vision for the flourishing and thriving of their community. This moves way beyond selfish individualism and congregationalism that has dominated the Western Church for too long.

How do we join in?

1. *What does 'good' look like in your local community?*

2. *How can you express the Kingdom of God through your actions in the workplace?*

3. *If your city was to adopt a Jesus culture where could you start?*

4. *What would it mean for you to love your country well?*

9

Participative Society

Abraham will surely become a great and powerful nation, and all nations on earth will be blessed through him.
(Genesis 18:18)

What is God doing?

Any cursory read of the Bible shows that God is not only interested in individuals, families and communities but also in societies and nations. In the Old Testament God chose Israel as a nation, not to exclude other nations from his love and purposes, but so that through the example of Israel other nations would be drawn to God and his people and be blessed by them. In the New Testament Jesus instructs us to, "go make disciples of all nations" (Matthew 28:19) which includes every nation, tribe, language and people. His purpose for these people is 'the healing of the nations' (Revelation 22:2).

The Western Church, in all its glorious ultra-individualism, often misinterprets this instruction as 'discipling individuals in different countries' rather than the discipling and transformation of whole nations. God is the nation builder whose purpose is to love and be loved by all the nations of the earth.

After the turn of the last century the UK government launched the welfare state with the introduction of minimum wage levels. The aftermath of the First World War led the state to become more involved in people's lives via the rationing of food and clothing and a commitment to ensuring full employment for all, free universal secondary education and the introduction of family allowances.

During the Second World War, the extensive influence of state control led people to believe that the state might be able to solve national social problems. The liberal economist William Beveridge published a report in 1942 identifying five giant evils of society: want, ignorance, squalor, disease and idleness and so recommended the provision of health care, unemployment and retirement benefits as a means by which to defeat them. It was soon after this that the National Health Service was formed in 1948 with the founding principles of comprehensive, universal and free healthcare at the point of delivery. Hospitals were not built but existing church and charity-based provision was nationalised in order to increase standardisation.

Beveridge believed that as people became healthier, the number of treatments and therefore the amount it cost to provide them would decrease. The opposite in fact has happened and the cost of the NHS has risen by an average of 4% per annum since. Within three years of the creation of the NHS the Labour government began introducing charges for specific services such as dentures and spectacles in order to try and manage the growing costs.

Through the emergence of the British Welfare State, church schools, hospitals and orphanages were nationalised and handed over to the State for ownership and control. In effect, the Church at this time stepped away from its social responsibility. Today a great reversal is taking place where, once again, the Church and other voluntary organisations are taking social responsibility for those people most at need in our nation. This has now been encouraged by successive British Prime Ministers.

On 19th July 2010 Prime Minister David Cameron launched his vision for a 'Big Society' with great passion and vision as the big idea for his premiership. The idea was focused on creating a smaller state and a bigger society spearheaded by the reform of public services and a greater involvement of the voluntary and community sectors. It was this speech that inspired me to start Cinnamon Network to activate the UK Church in playing a bigger part in society.

At the same time Cameron was announcing major spending cuts across public and welfare services. He was criticised by the opposition Labour party and the media for making people's lives more difficult whilst asking them to do more. So slowly but surely 'big society' visionary rhetoric faded from the spotlight and by the end of his premiership in 2016 it was virtually non-existent.

Prime Minister Theresa May has also laid out her vision for the nation and wrote in The Telegraph newspaper (8 January 2017), "So when you see others prospering while you are not; when you try to raise your concerns but they fall on deaf ears; when you feel locked out of the political and social discourse and feel no one is on your side, resentments grow, and the divisions that we see around us – between a more prosperous older generation and a struggling younger generation; between the wealth of London and the rest of the country; between the rich, the successful and the powerful, and their fellow citizens – become entrenched."

May continued, "Overcoming these divisions and bringing our country together is the central challenge of our time. That means building the shared society. A society that doesn't just value our individual rights but focuses rather more on the responsibilities we have to one another; a society that respects the bonds of family, community, citizenship and strong institutions that we share as a union of people and nations; a society with a commitment to fairness at its heart."

So what was 'big society' under Cameron has become 'shared society' under May. In essence, what both leaders are setting out is what I would call a vision for a 'participative society' where every person is loved, valued and celebrated, and also encouraged to make their voice heard and take responsibility for playing a full part in our common life together. In a participative society, citizens not only take responsibility for themselves and their family but for their community and nation.

The fact that British Prime Ministers are talking in this way creates an incredible historic opportunity for the Church to help reshape our nation's social contract and once again to take greater social responsibility for the wellbeing of our country. It does however, mean that we need to distance our self from ultra-individualism and extreme nationalism, which threaten to undermine our God-given calling to serve the nation.

The Archbishop of Canterbury Justin Welby and the Archbishop of Westminster Cardinal Vincent Nichols wrote in a report 'Doing Good' about the importance of civil society explaining, 'Periods of predominance of the state or, alternatively, of the market, have revealed the weakness of both, sometimes with dire consequences. Increasingly, politicians and commentators across the political spectrum are realising that a good society desperately needs a third element if it is to be truly healthy. This element, sometimes known as civil society, is one in which people come together and serve simply for the sake of service, recognising a common humanity. It is an element in which the Church has long dwelt and one in which it continues today to demonstrate the unquenchable love of God on an enormous scale.' At the heart of participative society is a sense of collectivism, service and self-giving to others.

Churches in other nations are already stepping up in this way. Despite the fact that there is little or no state welfare provision in Africa, I'm always impressed by the family welfare model that operates across the continent, whereby people who do well generously help and support those within their extended family and community who need assistance. Like the UK state welfare system, the African approach is far from perfect – but it is a powerful example of social responsibility in action.

It is interesting that both David Cameron and Theresa May have publicly declared that they are Christians. Cameron described his faith as a little like listening to Radio 4 in the Cotswolds, in that it fades in and out from time to time. May, on the other hand, is the daughter of the Manse and has spoken with great conviction about how her faith helps her make difficult decisions.

When a church builds a relationship with its community and civic institutions to serve the poor it becomes part of participative society and serves the nation. This is exactly what Cinnamon Network helps churches do and is a direct response to Christ, who said, "Whoever wants to be my disciple must deny themselves and take up their cross daily and follow me. For whoever wants to save their life will lose it, but whoever loses their life for me will save it. What good is it for someone to gain the whole world, and yet lose or forfeit their very self?" (Luke 9:23-25 NIV). Meaning in life is not found in what you get, but in what you give.

Pushing against this ideal are some unpleasant forces at work in our nations that draw on the uncertain times we're living in to create a sense of fear that leads to ultra-individualism and extreme nationalism. The UK European Union Referendum and the election of President Donald Trump, along with the rise of the far right across Europe, can be interpreted as acts of selfish nationalism. The fear of immigration and a desire to control national borders are driving forces behind them all and have pushed us further away from the ideas of participative society.

It's concerning to see how some politicians have manipulated our innate drive for self-preservation on a national scale. Nigel Farage, leader of UKIP at the time of Brexit (the UK's Referendum on being part of the European Union), stoked the fire of fear within many when he said, "Theresa May says it's difficult to control immigration as part of the EU. She's wrong – it's not difficult, it's impossible". In the US, President Donald Trump appealed to the sense of self-preservation with his mantra "America First." Within 10 days of taking office he issued executive orders for a wall to be built between Mexico and the United States and set about a ban on the entry of citizens from a number of Muslim majority countries. Extreme nationalism, by its very nature, is selfish rather than selfless.

The problem is that fundamentally we all find self-interest easier than selflessness. When God asked Cain, "Where is your brother Abel?" he responded with the question, "Am I my brother's keeper?" (Genesis 4:9). I believe what Cain should have said is, "I am responsible for my brother." We need individuals, families, communities, cities and nations that take responsibility to unselfishly look out for each other. Let's build people, cities and nations that are less selfishly individualistic and more socially responsible – a truly participative society.

How do we join in?

1. *If your life were to be audited how much evidence would there be that you are your brother's keeper?*

2. *How committed is your place of work to social responsibility?*

3. *What could be done to achieve a better balance between our rights and our responsibilities?*

4. *How do we save ourselves from ultra-individualism or extreme nationalism?*

5. *What do you believe is God's vision for your nation and how are you joining in?*

10

Numbers Speak Louder Than Words

> *The Lord spoke to Moses in the tent of meeting in the Desert of Sinai on the first day of the second month of the second year after the Israelites came out of Egypt. He said: "Take a census of the whole Israelite community by their clans and families, listing every man by name, one by one."*
> (Numbers 1:1-2)

What is God doing?

As the Church we are particularly great at telling stories because we are led by preachers who spend their lives engaging with people through telling powerful narratives that connect on a personal level. As most organisations reflect the personality of their leaders so, in turn, we as congregations are also story tellers. I believe God is helping his Church learn to speak in numbers as well as stories so that we can communicate the value of what we do to local authorities, police forces and other agencies. If we want to take seriously the challenge of working with others, then we need to learn to speak in their language, which is so often quantitative. I'm not suggesting that we give up with storytelling, we just need to become ambidextrous and use both stories and numbers to give a much more complete picture of what we do.

I was invited to speak at a special event being hosted at Chester Cathedral with the Bishop, Chief Executive of local authority and a senior police officer. The occasion was the publishing of their Faith Action Audit 2013, which was an update of their Faith Action Audit 2010 that assessed the quantitative impact faith organisations in the area made to the community. In the three years between the audits, there had been a 13% increase in the number of community projects, 20% increase in the number of volunteers and 54% increase in the number of individuals benefitting from services provided by churches and faith-based organisations. The value of the time given by churches across these community projects was worth nearly £3 million to the West Cheshire economy.

Stoke-on-Trent also undertook a Faith Action Audit in 2008 thanks to a city-wide leader Lloyd Cooke. When the Chief Executive of the City Council read the Faith Action Audit results he was delighted. One of the areas of surprise was that local churches in the city were doing twice as much work amongst the elderly as any other agency. Consequently, the council made a grant to the churches to co-ordinate and develop this important work. The point isn't that funding was released, but that civic organisations were enabled to see the value of what churches are doing and pursue opportunities to work with them in new ways.

The excellent examples of the Faith Action Audits in Chester and Stoke-on-Trent inspired Cinnamon Network to create a Faith Action Audit model that could be undertaken by multiple cities across the UK. The invitation to churches in cities across the UK received a huge response, in 2014-2015 a total of fifty-seven cities took part and in 2015-2016 a further thirty. It is the most comprehensive faith action research of its kind ever undertaken.

In our approach, we took a risk in asking churches to survey the work of all faith groups, not just churches and Christian organisations. It was important that civic leaders reviewing the research saw that we were inclusive in our approach and that this wasn't merely a piece of Christian propaganda. Of course, we took into consideration the multiple sensitivities around faiths as I shall explore in Chapter 11.

In total, Cinnamon Faith Action Audit UK approached 6,537 local churches and other faith groups and an incredible 3,007, which was 46%, responded. The industry standard for market research suggests that if you get a response rate in double figures you are doing incredibly well, so by this standard our response rate was outstanding and certainly ensured our findings were accurate. This was in most part thanks to the incredible hard work of the Cinnamon Faith Action Audit champions who volunteered locally to encourage groups to respond to the survey.

In total, the local churches and other faith groups that responded were generating 197,634 volunteer roles and employing 12,789 people to provide 5.1 million moments when a community beneficiary was helped. The value of the time given by local churches and faith groups in the survey was worth over £319 million. This was then extrapolated across the UK making headlines in The Times newspaper who reported, "Loving thy neighbour is priceless – but it's also worth £3 billion". There is no denying that the UK Church is making an astonishing contribution to the social economy.

Archbishop Justin Welby spoke at the launch of our Cinnamon Faith Action Audit results and said, "The public view of religion among young people, according to a YouGov poll, is that 41% of 18-24 year olds agreed that 'religion is more often the cause of evil in the world' and only 14% say it is a cause for good. The Cinnamon Faith Action Audit reveals something different. It shows the breadth of commitment across the country, the depth of commitment, and above all the strength of experience and good practice. Thanks to Cinnamon and other bodies like it, this is not mere do-goodery. It is seeking to find best practice and put it into action in the most professional way that can be imagined."

I recently spoke at the launch of the Cinnamon Faith Action Audit Cambridge. Results from the audit showed that faith-based organisations ran 527 projects, created 4,762 volunteer roles and supported 89,658 community beneficiaries. The value of the time given to the community was worth £8.4 million a year. The civic leaders present were overwhelmed by the scale and reach of the work of the churches and other faith based groups. Gillian Beasley, Chief Executive of Cambridgeshire County Council in response to hearing the numbers said, "Churches are closer to communities than statutory agencies can ever be". As a result of that audit alone Cinnamon is exploring partnership with both the council and the police in Cambridge to support more churches in the county as they engage effectively with their communities.

In the London borough of Haringey officials produced a community plan where the only mention of the local church was in a section about mitigating extremism. Church leaders were concerned about the false impression this gave, so they asked for a meeting with the Chief Executive of the local government and the leader of the council where they produced their Cinnamon Faith Action Audit as evidence of the positive impact that local churches and other faith groups were having in the community. The church leaders are now working much more closely with the local government to ensure that churches are part of the wider community plan.

At the launch of the Cinnamon Faith Action Audit in Lincoln, not only were churches challenged to work with local government, they were also challenged to work together with one another in a new way. The leader of the council explained that if they could work together as one, the city council could then look to truly partner with them. As a result, the Lincoln Active Faith Network was formed as a conduit to help the city churches and the city council to work closely together. Civic partnerships often require that churches get more organised and have a single point of contact to enable more proactive communication.

Of course, the proof of the pudding, as they say, is in the eating, so here at Cinnamon we also commissioned research to assess the effectiveness of police and church partnerships. The research looked at the city of Chichester in the south of England where, on a Friday and Saturday night, trained volunteers from churches across the city work closely with the police and local businesses. Under the banner of City Angels, they help to diffuse tension, provide practical support and sometimes just offer a listening ear to the city's revelers.

According to Sussex Police crime data, on a Saturday night when the Angels are on patrol anti-social behaviour is reduced by 79%, violent crime by 50% and violent crime leading to injury by 82%. The results really do speak for themselves. The research was endorsed by both the College of Policing and the National Police Chiefs Council. It has resulted in a number of police forces partnering with Cinnamon Network to support local churches in delivering similar results in other communities.

After reading this research Armagh local authority in Northern Ireland contacted Cinnamon and asked to meet. They too were facing challenges of antisocial behaviour and violent crime around the night time economy. Despite their best efforts, they hadn't been able to address the challenges and neither had the police, so they were looking for a new way of working and wondered if church and police partnerships could be the answer. Inspired by City Angels, the churches met together and are now taking steps to work with the local authority to replicate the model.

When the Church learns to speak in numbers as well as stories the value of what we do in communities can be understood more clearly. Numbers give the churches a new confidence about the value of impact it has and numbers give civic organisations a new confidence about the value churches can bring. When churches and civic organisations see the numbers they are often as surprised as each other! Cinnamon has proved that new confidence leads to new conversations and new levels of collaboration between churches and civic organisations.

As we look ahead Cinnamon is developing quantitative evidence to show the impact that churches have when they work with other civic authorities, such as health services. We know stories where local churches have helped people with mental health difficulties, transformed well-being and looked after patients at home, but stories alone aren't enough. We need numbers to prove impact. Only when we can speak about these things with an evidence base will health services become more interested in proactively partnering with local churches and local church networks to address health inequalities.

How do we join in?

1. *How could your church better measure changed-lives in the community?*

2. *What would it take for your city to undertake a Cinnamon Faith Action Audit to measure the value of the contribution made by churches to the community each year?*

3. *Which civic organisations would your church like to partner with and what evidence might convince them to do so?*

4. *Inputs and outputs are most easily measured but how could you measure outcomes?*

11

Salt and Pepper

> *So in Christ Jesus you are all children of God through faith, for all of you who were baptised into Christ have clothed yourselves with Christ. There is neither Jew nor Gentile, neither slave nor free, nor is there male and female, for you are all one in Christ Jesus.*
> (Galatians 3:26-28)

What is God doing?

Even in this day and age, local churches in the United Kingdom, United States and South Africa, for example, are often tragically segregated into black and white. God is moving the global Church to become less ethnically segregated and more ethnically integrated and diverse.

'No Irish, No Blacks, No Dogs' were the signs that greeted Irish and Caribbean immigrants in the UK well into the 1960s. I have Caribbean friends whose parents and siblings lived through this abominable time in British history and remember first-hand the stories of racism. The British Church behaved no better than British society and their racism was one of the factors that led to the emergence of black-led and black-majority churches.

Now zoom forwards to 2016 and the fundamental problem remains. The think tank Open Democracy published a report claiming that Britain is increasingly racially segregated. Based on research from the 2001 and 2011 national census, white and minority ethnic communities are "increasingly polarised" in urban areas and big cities. Areas that have a large percentage of ethnic minorities have dwindling white populations. Professor Eric Kaufmann and Prof Ted Cantle explained that England has become more diverse but areas with large minority ethnic communities have become less diverse. This is the result of what is known as 'white flight' or 'white avoidance', where, as communities have become more diverse the white communities have moved out. So the United Kingdom continues to struggle with racial integration.

At its worst this is racism, which British society has never managed to rid itself of. People who are explicitly racist are easy to spot and, I believe, frankly evil. But what is also concerning, and I would argue even more dangerous, is prejudice. This ingrained sense of superiority is held by many very intelligent people and is subtler and more discreet but no less evil than racism.

Black and white divisions continue to blight communities across the world, whether it be in the United Kingdom, the

United States or South Africa. The ability of communities to hold themselves together and to become increasingly integrated rather than increasingly fragmented and segregated is one of the greatest challenges facing our world today.

But it is not all bad news. We do have a powerful history of black and white working together towards social reform. In the late 17th and early 18th centuries the abolitionist movement worked to end the practice of slavery. White people such as the politician William Wilberforce and his friends who became known as the Clapham Sect or the Clapham Saints, worked alongside black people such as former slave Olaudah Equiano in order to bring an end to the abominable transatlantic slave trade.

I remember attending an event to mark the bicentenary of the end of the transatlantic slave trade where the special guest was the Prime Minister of the day. As I looked across the room I spotted an Afro-Caribbean guy who clearly loved tie and pocket square combinations as much as I did. Later that evening we managed to find each other in the crowd and became what Americans call 'fast friends'. Instead of going out for the traditional get-to-know-each-other-over-lunch, we went tie and pocket square shopping.

Early on in our friendship we covenanted to introduce one another to each other's worlds. I remember taking him to political events and wine tastings. Afterwards he would say how much fun he had had and then joked with me that the event had been a "white wash" because he was the only non-white face in the room. He would then take me to restaurants and parties and afterwards I would joke with him that the event had been a "black out" because I was the only non-black face in the room. We realised our worlds looked very little like the picture of heaven described throughout Revelation where 'every people, tribe and language' are gathered. We have since become incredibly enriched by knowing each other through the places we've been, the people we've met and the way our minds have been expanded.

It's not always been easy to accommodate each other and we still work hard at our friendship, but getting to know people who are different to us is both a challenge and an opportunity. Our journey of discovery continues and one of these days we are going to write a book together called *Salt and Pepper: the journey of two friends and their very different worlds*. The thing is we all have to work hard at friendship, no matter what the circumstances. So my advice to anyone embarking on a cross cultural friendship would be to simply do all the things you would normally do to build a friendship and don't be afraid of what is new and different.

Start by being adventurous. Ask friends to take you to places that you wouldn't normally go and to meet people who you wouldn't normally meet. Throw yourself in and absorb as much as you possibly can. Secondly, be curious. Spend time together offline, when no-one else is around, when you can ask your friend as many questions as you can with the main aim of trying to understand more than being understood. Finally, be flexible. This is the time to break out of your 'normal' frame of mind and create lots of 'soft edges'. If you live with brittle boundaries, you can expect some of them to break.

One sector of society that has struggled with racial tension is the police. In 1993 a young black man named Stephen Lawrence was murdered in a racially motivated attack in south east London. The police handling of the case was subject to an investigation and the 1999 Macpherson report concluded that the Metropolitan Police was 'institutionally racist'. The Met Police continue to struggle to address institutional racism today. In 2011 Mark Duggan, an unarmed black man, was fatally shot by police which resulted in riots across London. Those from ethnic minorities are subjected to high rates of 'stop and search' and black people and those from other ethnic minorities appear to have their careers limited to junior ranks. Whilst the Met Police do an incredible job in keeping London and its millions of citizens safe, the issue of institutional racism is something that still needs to be eradicated.

One of my best friends, who I discussed this chapter with, said that when a white person is stopped by the police they ask themselves, "What have I done wrong?" But when a black person is stopped they ask themselves, "What is going to be done to me?" Policing is not the only institution that is guilty of racism, there are times when we all need to take a long hard look at ourselves.

The United States police also struggle with institutional racism. In 2014 Michael Brown an unarmed black 18-year-old was fatally shot by a white officer in Ferguson, Missouri. In a predominantly black city protests and civil unrest erupted. More recently in 2016 Charles Kinsey, another unarmed black man was shot by a white officer. The President, Barak Obama, spoke out to try and quell the unrest saying, "What is true for a lot of African American men is there's a greater presumption of dangerousness that arises from the social and cultural perceptions that have been fed to folks for a long time," adding, "But black folks and Latino folks also carry some assumptions. You may see a police officer who's doing everything right, and you already assumed the worst rather than the best in him, and we have to guard against that as well."

Policing styles vary around the world. The United States like many countries have a paramilitary style of law enforcement, whereby officers carry firearms. By contrast the United Kingdom approach is based on policing by consent and an understanding that the police are the public and the public are the police. It's built on the assumption that the police are only members of the public who are paid to give attention to what every citizen is committed to – namely building stronger and safer communities. Sir Robert Peel who was Home Secretary in the 19th century is regarded as the father and architect of modern British policing. He created nine principles of policing, which have subsequently become known as the Peelian Principles and are the foundations of ethical policing by consent. The British approach to policing is renowned and respected across the globe and its senior officers are often involved in the development of other police forces around the world.

Regardless of policing style, it is critically important that all police forces have good relationships with the community. This is helped when the police reflect the diversity and ethnicity of the communities they serve. It's a principal which is equally true for every organisation and network. However, we can often fool ourselves into seeing diversity where there is none. Recently I attended an international gathering with representatives from many of the world's 196 nations. A group of five people were introduced as the 'new leadership'. When they described themselves as 'diverse' I nearly laughed out loud; they were all white, old, middle class men. I have nothing against white, old, middle class men – but don't insult our intelligence by describing yourselves as diverse.

Professor of Sociology at Texas State University, Barbara Trepagnier in her book *Silent Racism: How well-meaning white people perpetuate the racial divide* argues that we are all racist because we are all wrestling with prejudice. She says that we should always interrupt racism, whether comments or behaviour, because to ignore racism is to collude with racism. We should even interrupt 'granny' who in another era we might have ignored, knowing she was brought up at a time when those comments might have been the norm. If racism is allowed to continue uninterrupted and unchecked, it can become part of our culture and even part of our institutions. Trepagnier suggests those who are most racially aware are those who have strong relationships with people of other ethnicity. These should be egalitarian relationships where there is no power disparity and where the tough issues are talked about.

Recently I was discussing racial justice with an Indian friend who had converted to Christianity from Hinduism. He explained what it was like to be brought up within the Indian caste system and how it had created a latent racism within him that he was still having to work through. The more I think about it, the more I think that Trepagnier is right and that we are all dealing with our own innate racism and prejudice.

If we look to the Bible for inspiration, then we can see Jesus, on numerous occasions, confronting racial hatred of his time. A racial enmity existed between Jews and Samaritans that dated back six hundred years. The Samaritans had opposed the Jews who were rebuilding Jerusalem and also built a temple where they worshipped false gods. Consequently, if you were a Jew you hated Samaritans on racial grounds. Jesus, however, made a point of interacting with Samaritans very publicly. We have plenty of examples, such as the Samaritan woman at the well (John 4) and the story of the Good Samaritan (Luke 10), which Jesus used to challenge Jewish leaders about their hypocrisy and racial injustice by presenting a Samaritan as the hero.

Given the increasing diversity of most communities, cities and countries ethnically diverse leadership is a 'must have' requirement not a 'nice to have'. Churches, public sector, not for profit and for profit organisations and networks that have ethnically diverse leadership are more effective, innovative and productive – they have the ability to think differently, behave differently and deliver differently.

How do we join in?

1. *If you were to have a racist moment who are you most likely to be prejudiced about?*

2. *What are the racial injustices that exist within your community, city and country?*

3. *How ethnically diverse is the leadership of your church and what positive action could you take to make it more diverse?*

4. *If people from other ethnicities and cultures were to look at your organisation, would they be able to see themselves?*

5. *How ethnically diverse is your workplace and what positive action could you take to make it more diverse?*

6. *How could you increase your organisation or network's effectiveness, innovation and productivity by increasing the diversity of your leadership and teams?*

12

Distinctive Faiths

Therefore, if anyone is in Christ, the new creation has come: the old has gone, the new is here! All this is from God, who reconciled us to himself through Christ and gave us the ministry of reconciliation.
(2 Corinthians 5:17-18)

What is God doing?

For decades many Churches have resisted involvement with other faiths because they rightly believe in the uniqueness of Christ – that Jesus is the only way to God and engaging with other faiths may be a distraction unless you are trying to convert them. God is calling his Church to build good relationships with people of other faiths for the benefit of the harmony, peace and well-being of our communities, cities and countries.

The 9/11 attacks by Muslim extremists on the United States changed modern history. On 11 September 2001 four passenger airliners were hijacked, two were flown into the twin towers of the World Trade Centre in New York, another into the Pentagon and another headed for Washington DC where it crashed into a field. The attacks killed 2,996 people and injured 6,000 others. Terrorists motivated by religious extremism, who had no care for the value of their own lives, were now unleashed on the world like we have never known before.

On 7 July 2005 four Muslim extremists deonated rucksacks packed with explosives during central London rush hour. Three were exploded on underground trains and one on a double decker bus, they killed fifty-two people and injured 700. It was the day after London had won the bid to host the 2012 Olympic Games – a process which had highlighted what a diverse and multicultural city London really was.

I felt compelled to pick up the telephone and speak to a Muslim friend who was a leading figure at the local mosque in South West London, which happens to be the largest in Europe. We agreed that, at this time of great volatility, it was critically important for Christian and Muslim communities to build good relationships. So we agreed to arrange a reciprocal visit between our two communities.

Interfaith has been encouraged by United Kingdom governments for many years and this has increased significantly since the rise in religious extremism. Unfortunately, I believe it's no more than a PR strategy. The premise of interfaith is universalist – that all faiths are the same really, so why don't they work more closely together. The liberal ends of any of the faith traditions will engage because they are the only ones that believe that they are all the same really. The orthodox and fundamental ends of each faith tradition believe in the uniqueness of their faith as the only path to God. So they will never engage in the interfaith agenda because they can't agree with the starting point, let alone where it might end up. Religious extremism doesn't exist off the end of liberalism but off the end of fundamentalism, so interfaith is a waste of time, energy and resources as a religious extremism mitigation strategy.

This kind of state intervention in the lives and beliefs of individuals and communities will always be a little clumsy. In the United Kingdom, the government has initiated what has become known as the 'Prevent' programme as part of their counter-terrorism strategy. It has caused huge controversy. Whilst the aim of the initiative is to make society more vigilant and responsible, it has also driven the growth of a surveillance culture, where, for example, teachers are obliged to report children whose families they suspect of engaging in terrorist activity. One child's home was raided when his teacher thought that he said that he lived in a "terrorist house". The child actually said that he lived in a "terraced house". My point is not that seeking intelligence is wrong, but that grassroots community solutions will always be more effective than those imposed from the top.

Following the 7/7 London bombings I proposed to my Muslim friend that we did not describe what we were going to do as an interfaith visit. Instead we positioned our initiative as a distinctive faith visit. We started with the assumption that there were significant differences in our beliefs and through the visit we sought to explore and understand those differences. So I drew together a group of thirty church leaders and visited the mosque. We invited our hosts to tell us about the distinctives of Islam. A group of the Muslim leaders then visited one of the churches and they invited us to talk to them about the distinctives of Christianity. Even the most conservative and reformed within our Christian community took part in the visit because it was not interfaith. The dialogue was fresh, enlightening and open. Both groups had an opportunity to speak about what was important to them, rather than skirting round the main issues for fear of offending.

On 14 July 2016 in the French city of Nice, eighty-four people were killed, including children, after a lorry slammed into a crowd celebrating Bastille day. The driver ploughed through the crowds for 1.2 miles and witnesses reported him swerving and zig zagging as he attempted to cause the maximum number of fatalities. In recent years the intensity of Muslim extremists committing terrorist atrocities in France has increased dramatically from one incident in 2013, to three in 2014, six in 2015 and five in 2016. Recently I was asked to speak at the French Evangelical Alliance General Assembly. The group were interested in exploring how churches could begin to address the issue of religious extremism and radicalisation – no small task. This is not natural ground for evangelicals but thankfully it is now increasingly seen as a priority.

One of the greatest challenges for our world at this time is facing up to religious extremism and radicalisation. Young men and women of a Muslim faith who find themselves living in an alien culture where they are segregated and marginalised can feel socially and culturally isolated. This leaves them vulnerable to religious extremism that offers a certainty and a counter narrative where they become the hero. The problem is compounded by the fact that more often than not, the process of radicalisation takes place online so it is very difficult to actively prevent.

There are other issues of global concern that the church also needs to stand up and address. When our world became more aware of the true extent of the environmental impact that humanity was having on the planet and began to develop campaigns to change policies and behaviours, the global Church sadly found itself on the back foot. Given the Church's understanding of God as the creator who gave us stewardship of the planet, we really should have been leading the pack. Thankfully we have caught up, but there are many other issues that I would love to see the Church leading on.

Wouldn't it be amazing if the global Church could set an example when it comes to challenging religious extremism and radicalisation? I'm not suggesting we are the whole solution, but we could certainly play a part. Christianity is one of Islam's nearest neighbours. Like Judaism we are Abrahamic faiths who can trace our origins to the great Patriarch Abraham.

Abraham and his wife Sarah struggled to have children and so Sarah suggested that her servant, Hagar, could bear Abraham's child, and so Ishmael was born. Later Abraham and Sarah conceived their own son, Isaac. Understandably this caused some tensions between Sarah and Hagar and subsequently their two sons. The tension came to a head over the issue of inheritance. 'Abraham left everything he owned to Isaac. But while he was still living, he gave gifts to the sons of his concubines and sent them away from his son Isaac to the land of the east' (Genesis 25:5-6). Notice that Abraham's sons from his servants, including Ishmael, were sent away from Isaac to the east so as not to threaten his son's succession. Despite the tensions, both sons buried their father, 'His sons Isaac and Ishmael buried him' (Genesis 25:9). It is interesting that the Ishmaelites were those who 'rescued' Joseph from death when his brothers sold him in slavery (Genesis 37:27-28) and, as a result, saved the people from starvation (Genesis 45:4-5).

The lineage of Judaism and Christianity can be traced to Abraham's son Isaac and the lineage of Islam to Abraham's son Ishmael. Despite our differences as people of Abrahamic faith we have an understanding of one another. We will need to find a way to navigate around the interfaith agenda and develop alternative approaches that appreciate the distinctiveness of what we believe.

Co-belligerence is the name given to groups who work together for a common objective despite significant religious, cultural or ideological differences. For example, co-belligerence was used during the latter stages of the Second World War to define the status of former German allies, like Italy, after they joined the Allied war against Germany. There was a limited operational co-ordination that took place between them. Another example is evident in the way Nelson Mandela behaved when during his final years in captivity he met with those who were responsible for his incarceration to discuss positive outcomes for South Africa.

Whilst Christians may disagree with Muslims and those of other faiths it should not stop us from working together, even in a limited way, to overcome religious extremism for the benefit of building peaceful communities. Archbishop of Canterbury Justin Welby has made reconciliation one of his three priorities explaining, "Reconciliation doesn't mean we all agree. It means we find ways of disagreeing – perhaps very passionately – but loving each other deeply at the same time, and being deeply committed to each other. That's the challenge for the church if we are actually going to speak to our society, which is increasingly divided in many different ways."

It may seem like a contradiction in terms to work alongside those whose core beliefs we disagree with, but then the Bible is full of seemingly impossible situations and circumstances that are made possible with God.

Whatever is done to initiate, maintain and strengthen mutually respectful relationships between individuals, families and religious communities can only be a very good thing. We will never experience transformation in our communities, cities and countries until we learn to live well with people who are different to us and with whom we disagree.

How do we join in?

1. *What would happen if followers of Jesus began to build more relationships with people of other faiths?*

2. *What could your church, or local church network, do to build stronger positive relationships of respect with people of other faiths?*

3. *How could you encourage more ethnically mixed relationships in your community, city or country?*

4. *Could you reach out to Muslim people in your community who may feel socially and culturally isolated?*

5. *Is there a local church community project that addresses social cohesion and anti-extremism that you could let Cinnamon Network know about as a potentially replicable project?*

13

Outrageous Generosity

Remember this: Whoever sows sparingly will also reap sparingly, and whoever sows generously will also reap generously. Each of you should give what you have decided in your heart to give, not reluctantly or under compulsion, for God loves a cheerful giver. And God is able to bless you abundantly, so that in all things at all times, having all that you need, you will abound in every good work.
(2 Corinthians 9:6-8)

What is God doing?

It often makes me sad when Christianity and indeed Christians are characterised as stingy because God is completely the opposite. God is outrageously generous and calls us to be outrageously generous also.

Jesus said the Kingdom of Heaven is like a vineyard owner who went out early in the morning to hire workers to pick that year's harvest of grapes. He agreed to pay those workers a denarius. It must have been a bumper vintage because the vineyard owner kept returning to the marketplace throughout the day to hire more pickers, at 9am, 12noon, 3pm and 5pm. At the end of the day the vineyard owner told his foreman to pay the workers starting with those hired last. Each worker, regardless of when they were hired, was paid a denarius. The rumbling, murmuring and grumbling began as soon as the workers realised they had all been paid the same. Those who were hired first were paid what they were promised as were those who were hired last. You can almost hear the unions rallying troops; this was outrageous. The story culminated with the words of the vineyard owner: "Are you envious because I am generous" (Matthew 20:1-16).

The vineyard owner is, of course, God portrayed with an outrageously generous character and personality. His generosity is outrageous because God gives to all of us even though we don't deserve it. There is none among us who merit or deserve God's love, kindness and generosity, but he gives anyway because that is his nature. He is a God of unconditional love and grace.

In 2014 the BBC commissioned research about British attitudes to giving and it showed that Christians are more generous givers than people who do not claim to hold the faith. As the broadcaster wanted to find a 'Christian voice' to respond to the research, I was whisked in an executive car to the BBC and sat in a broom cupboard-sized radio studio for a couple of hours answering questions and giving comment to more than a dozen BBC radio stations. As you can imagine, the radio presenters were looking for me to say something contentious. After a few arrow prayers I had a plan; when the presenter asked me why did I think Christian's were more generous I responded, "Christians are more generous not because they are better people but because God is generous and they are trying to follow him".

As a child I don't remember being taught about money. I've picked it up as I've gone along. Consequently, I'm trying hard to teach my own three children about being responsible and generous with their finances. My children have three piggy banks: one for spending, another for saving and a third for sharing. Each week I give them a minimum of three coins and they must put a minimum of one coin in each piggy bank – they are free to do what they like with any other coins they may have. One of my children is a real spender (like their dad), another is a diligent saver and is already saving for their first home and my third child often puts the most money in their sharing piggy bank – something which I think is outrageously generous.

Across the world there are stories of Christians living outrageously generous lives, which are an inspiration to us all. The Power of Half is the story of the Salwen family from Atlanta, Georgia and their teenage daughter Hannah who suggested they sell their home and give half the money away. In 2006, after much discussion and wrestling, that is exactly what the family decided to do. They sold their house and downsized to one half the price and less than half the size. This released $850,000 which the family gave to a charity that helps lessen the hunger and increases the livelihoods of 30,000 individuals in more than thirty rural villages in Ghana – outrageous generosity.

I am grateful to have friends who role model outrageous generosity to me and my family. One great example is a couple I know from the United Kingdom who decided to celebrate their shared 50th birthdays in a slightly different way. They chose to celebrate a Biblical year of jubilee in which they gave away 100% of what they earned in their 50th year. It took some planning and saving but it meant that they could be outrageously generous. Another couple live by the stake in the ground principle. At the start of each financial year they decide how much money they are going to live on and then whatever they and their business earn over that amount they give away to charity. Another family have increased the percentage of their giving from a tithe to a reverse tithe, which means they give 90% of what they earn to the church and live off the remaining 10%.

One of my generosity heroes is Gary Grant, the owner of The Entertainer toy stores. He started his business in 1981 with one toyshop in Amersham, England and now has a network of over 120 stores as well as international franchises. Gary is passionate about being generous and encouraging others to be open hearted and open handed when it comes to giving. The business tithes its profits to a charity called Restore Hope, which works to meet the needs of underprivileged children and families. Staff are encouraged to be generous by offering them matched funding for any monies they give from their payroll to charity; an incredible 45% of the people take up this offer. Customers are also encouraged to be generous through the 'Pennies' initiative where people paying with credit or debit cards are given the opportunity to round up the value of the purchases to the nearest pound for charity. To date more than £1.2 million has been given in this way.

A few years ago a guy was introduced to me who spent his time visiting Christian charities working in the community and giving them money from his family's foundation. What a great job! His passion extended even further and he encouraged others to give generously towards Christian charities working in the community as well. Together we launched a 'Dragon's Den' or 'Shark Tank' style event for the benefit of small Christian community charities. We extended an open invitation to Christian community charities to write to us, on a maximum of one page, and request the opportunity to present at the event. We were swamped with requests and a selection panel had the unenviable challenge of choosing just five charities to present at the event.

We then invited our most generous friends to sit in the audience at the event, which was hosted at Coutts & Co private client bank on The Strand in London. Each charity was given just six minutes to pitch their community project and then had a further six minutes to take questions from the audience. At the end of the evening we paused, prayed and invited our guests to pledge a gift to one, or more, of the charities that presented. We held our breath to see if anyone would come forward. We were not disappointed. Coutts & Co. were the first to put their hand in their pocket to make a pledge. Our aim was to run 10 events over five years and raise £500,000 for charity. Through the outrageous generosity of God's people, we ended up raising more than £1 million.

More recently I found myself hosting an informal lunch for three other Christian grant making foundations in the UK. Three years on, there are now twenty-five foundations sat around the table all committed to building relationships, sharing best practice and exploring ways that we can work more collaboratively. The group is now known as the Christian Funders' Forum and the group individually gives more than £30 million to Christian mission every year. Each year we now host an annual awards ceremony to shine a spotlight on the very best in Christian mission in the UK and internationally. I partly tell this story because I think it is a powerful model that grant making foundations in other nations could develop – so I'm really hoping they might read this!

Being around people of significant wealth has taught me that meaning in life is found not in what you get but in what you give. As Jesus said, "For whoever wants to be my disciple must deny themselves and take up their cross every day and follow me. For whoever wants to save his own life will lose it, but whoever loses their life for me will save it. What good is it for someone to gain the whole world, and yet to lose or forfeit their very self?" (Luke 9:23-25) My experience is that people with significant amounts of money are more likely to lack a sense of purpose and people who have a significant sense of purpose are more likely to lack money. Personally I would trade money for purpose any day, however the ideal is to have both so you can resource your purpose!

Different cultures and nations have different attitudes to giving and philanthropy. In some European countries the government tax the population and fund the state Church – sometimes even paying the salaries of priests and pastors. This has led to a culture where financial giving, let alone outrageous generosity, is not normal within a church setting. There is an attitude that because you pay your taxes to enable the Church to look after people's souls and to enable the government to look after people's welfare, there is no need to give anything extra.

There are lots of challenges with this scenario. One of the biggest is in terms of individuals' mindsets toward financial giving – because people have already given to the Church through their taxes, they feel no compulsion to do so again. This sort of state-controlled giving also creates a false division between the care of souls and the care of people's welfare. In this scenario, the non-state or free churches miss out in every direction because they receive nothing from the state and they have to work twice as hard to teach and disciple people about financial giving. In other nations there is a total separation of Church and state and in those contexts followers of Jesus are naturally more attuned to their responsibility about financial giving.

Globally there is a growing movement of philanthropy. In 2010 Bill Gates and Warren Buffett announced The Giving Pledge campaign to inspire wealthy people to give the majority of their net profit to philanthropic causes during their lifetime or on their death. So far in excess of $732 billion has been pledged by 139 individuals. Among these are Mark Zuckerberg, founder of Facebook, and his wife Priscilla Chan who announced they would give away the majority of their wealth through the course of their lives. Their foundation to advance human potential and promote equality will receive 99% of their Facebook shares, worth $45 billion.

An international NGO recently claimed it was 'simply unacceptable' that the world's richest eight people had more wealth than the world's poorest half. The information they shared was correct, but through their presentation of the facts they insinuated that the rich are to blame for the huge problem of global poverty. In doing so, they not only failed to offer a solution, they also seemed to absolve the rest of us. It's worth noting that five of the eight billionaires named by the international charity have committed themselves to The Giving Pledge. These individuals should be celebrated and applauded. The Bible neither glamorises poverty or criminalises wealth. In fact, God made Solomon both the richest of all kings and also the wisest. What is of concern to God is not having wealth, but how we acquire it and what we do with it. 'The love of money,' we are told in 1 Timothy 6:10, is the root of all evil and not, as is commonly misquoted, merely having it.

Tom Hall the head of philanthropy at UBS UK recently spoke about the growth of performance philanthropy focused on the delivery of outcomes to end poverty. He explained that philanthropy can be used to catalyse innovation, generate evidence of outcomes and lead to collaboration with governments and business to scale the solution nationally or internationally. I was particularly struck that these solutions are part of a 20–30 year strategy. It is often said that you overestimate what you can achieve in a year but underestimate what you can achieve in ten years; I felt profoundly challenged to think about the strategy for my generosity over 20–30 years.

If we think again about Jesus' attitudes and behaviour, we can see that he is a wonderful disrupter of economics. The people who he cleansed and healed from leprosy were spiritually, physically and economically restored. They were once again allowed back into the temple to exercise their faith, they were included into society having left their commune and they were once again able to work for their livelihood rather than just begging. Jesus well and truly saved the lepers that he came into contact with.

At the other end of the spectrum, Jesus also hung out with a number of tax collectors. Perhaps the best known were the disciple Matthew and Zacchaeus, who Jesus called down from the tree. As a result of Zacchaeus' encounter with Jesus, the tax collector gave half of his earnings to the poor and anyone who he had cheated received a fourfold return (Luke 19:8).

The Apostle Peter visited the temple and saw a man, who had been unable to walk since birth, begging for money. He told the man, "Silver or gold I do not have, but what I do have I give to you. In the name of Jesus Christ of Nazareth, walk." (Acts 3:6). Jesus healed the man and transformed his body, his spirit and his economics – he could now walk and jump and work for, rather beg for, a living.

The coming Kingdom of God is outrageously generous. It not only blesses financially, but it creates and empowers people for employment and enterprise. As wisdom says, if you give a person a fish you feed them for a day, but if you teach them how to fish you feed them for a lifetime. Your greatest gift to people is not only to share your treasure with them but to help them find their own treasure. Systemic poverty can never be ended by charitable handouts – it can only be ended by applying our God-given minds to solve the root causes of poverty and create sustainable solutions that generate enterprise, create jobs and grow the economies of nations. If we are to see the transformation we long for in communities, cities and countries we are going to need to follow God's example of outrageous generosity in radical and entrepreneurial ways.

I wonder what would happen if we began to be more outrageously generous with what God has given us. What if we lived on less and gave more? What if we earned more and gave more? What if we optimised what we have and gave more? What could the impact be in our communities, cities and countries?

How do we join in?

1. *It is often said that your bank statement says more about your faith than the prayers you pray and the songs you sing. What does your bank statement say about your outrageous generosity?*

2. *What could you start to do today that would be outrageously generous to someone else?*

3. *What could you do to teach your children about money and being outrageously generous?*

4. *Besides financial giving, how else could you be outrageously generous with what God has given you?*

5. *How could your church show Christ to your city by being outrageously generous?*

6. *What difference could your business make to the country's economy?*

14

Unlikely Relationships

> *In your relationships with one another, have the same mindset as Christ Jesus: Who, being in very nature God, did not consider equality with God something to be used to his own advantage; rather, he made himself nothing by taking the very nature of a servant, being made in human likeness. And being found in appearance as a man, he humbled himself by becoming obedient to death – even death on a cross.*
> (Philippians 2:5-8)

What is God doing?

For decades the emphasis of leadership in Church and wider society has focused on position, status and power. You could get things done because of the title you held. Thankfully that has changed and leadership is increasingly all about influence, relationships and networks. God is increasingly leading his people to build unlikely relationships, partnerships and alliances to extend his Kingdom.

Nehemiah had the enviable job of being sommelier to King Artaxerxes (Nehemiah 1) and so at each meal he would choose appropriate wines to pair with the food and pour them for the King and his guests. In many ways it was bizarre that a lowly servant should have such a close relationship with royalty.

One day, King Artaxerxes noticed that Nehemiah was not himself and so he asked him what the matter was. Nehemiah explained that he had heard reports that his home city of Jerusalem lay in ruins, the city walls had been destroyed and the gates burnt. The King asked, "What is it you want?" so Nehemiah asked if he could be temporarily released from service and if the King would provide a letter of protection to enable him to travel safely. He also requested that the King provide him with a letter enabling Nehemiah to collect wood from the keeper of the royal parks. The King gave him all he asked and gave him an armed escort for his journey to Jerusalem as well. So Nehemiah returned to Jerusalem and with his collaborators rebuilt the walls and remade the gates – he restored his city.

It was an unlikely relationship but through it God was able to extend his Kingdom. Professor Mark Granovetter of Stanford University in the United States wrote a famous paper called 'The Strength of Weak Ties'. He described close relationships as strong ties and distant relationships as weak ties. Granovetter's research showed that strong ties tended to be homogenous relationships or with people that were like us, whereas weak ties tended to be heterogeneous relationships or with people who are unlike us.

He made the case for the strength of weak ties because whilst homogenous relationships are bonding relationships, heterogeneous relationships are bridging relationships that provide access to fresh ideas, opportunities and resources. Nehemiah's relationship with Artaxerxes was an unlikely bridging relationship that allowed him access to the King's resources. The King enabled Nehemiah to take leave from his work and gain the protection and resources he needed to fulfil what God had asked of him.

In many senses the entirety of this book is about what are sometimes perceived as unlikely relationships, partnerships and alliances. The chapter on 'De-Privatising Faith' is about unlikely relationships between church leaders and civic leaders and 'Stronger Together' explores unlikely relationships between church leaders of different denominations. 'Cultural Transformation' about the relationship between the church and the marketplace. 'Salt and Pepper' is about unlikely relationships between black leaders and white leaders and 'Distinctive Faiths' about unlikely relationships between followers of Jesus and people of other faiths.

The God of the Bible is a God of relationships. His fundamental identity is all about relationship; he is revealed as one God and three persons: the Father, Jesus Christ and the Holy Spirit. The Bible teaches us that we are created in his image and his likeness so we are also made for relationships. So God's primary way of working is through the relationships we build that enable the Holy Spirit to work. The greater the quality and quantity of relationships the more he can work.

The church that my family and I are a part of is Bless Community Church based in West London. The leader is Linda Ward who has been involved in starting a local church network across the London Borough of Ealing. As a charismatic community church leader she has co-led the local church network with an anglo-catholic parish priest called Father Andrew Davis. It has been an unlikely relationship and partnership that has been catalytic in bringing together church leaders from across every denomination, network and churchmanship. There is now a proposed shared building partnership emerging between the two churches – a truly unlikely relationship.

Cinnamon Network has built many unlikely relationships too. For example, the British Government launched a Social Action Fund to increase community philanthropy and volunteering and Cinnamon pitched an idea. Cinnamon would offer £2,000 micro-grants to local churches who would need to match fund the money in order to start a Cinnamon Recognised Project that would mobilise volunteers to take part in social action projects. So every £1 the British Government gave Cinnamon Network matched with £1 given by a local church. The funding was only given to new projects starting out, but the amazing thing was, 97% of the projects continued in to year two and 92% in to year three – even without the additional funding. The government was delighted with the results and invested more money in the programme. A national government funding a faith-based group to help local churches start community projects is an unlikely partnership, but it worked.

Cinnamon has also created an unlikely relationship with the British Police. College of Policing research has shown that 80% of emergency calls are not about crime, but rather welfare issues. Cinnamon has been able to demonstrate it can help local churches start community projects that reduce this welfare demand on police services, which in turn frees up police forces to focus on crime related issues. As a result, Cinnamon has multiple funding partnerships with police forces across the United Kingdom who fund Cinnamon to help local churches start community projects – another unlikely relationship.

Jesus extended the Kingdom of God not to the religious leaders but to those perceived to be on the margins of society and outside of God's care and concern. He built unlikely relationships with tax collectors, prostitutes, adulterers and Samaritans. When questioned by the chief priests Jesus said, "Truly I tell you, the tax collectors and the prostitutes are entering the Kingdom of God ahead of you. For John came to you to show you the way of righteousness, and you did not believe him, but the tax collectors and the prostitutes did. And even after you saw this, you did not repent and believe him" (Matthew 21:31-32). It was expected that the Messiah would build 'likely relationships' with religious leaders and not sinners and social outcasts. The example therefore for any follower of Jesus is to build unlikely relationships.

Throughout the Bible God has chosen to work through culturally unlikely relationships rather than the culturally likely ones. He has regularly chosen women over men, the old over the young, marketplace leaders over religious leaders, foreigners over nationals, small over large and sinners over the righteous.

Esther was a Jew who, being a virgin, was perhaps twelve or thirteen years old – and King Xerxes chose her to be his wife (Esther 2). As I mentioned in the introduction, when King Xerxes was advised to order the killing of all Jews, Esther cleverly influenced the King to recall the declaration of genocide before it was executed. God chose the unlikely relationship between a King and a young girl to save the genealogy that links Abraham through to David through to Jesus (Matthew and Luke).

I wonder what would happen if we began to build more unlikely relationships. Relationships with people that we strongly disagree with, relationships with people who we perceive to be our competitors, relationships with people who are our enemies and relationships with people who our church doesn't engage with. What unlikely relationships are we willing to build for the benefit of our communities, cities and countries?

We need to remember that God's ways are not our ways and our ways and not God's ways. Time and time again he has chosen the foolish things of this world to shame the wise, the unlikely things to surprise the likely. It's as if God is trying to make a point that it's not about us but about him. He will do what he wants, how he wants, whenever he wants in order to bring transformation in our communities, cities and countries.

How do we join in?

1. *How many unlikely relationships do you have?*

2. *Who are the people you would expect to find in your church community and who are the people that you would not expect to find?*

3. *How could you build more unlikely relationships to provide you with access to ideas, opportunities and resources that you might not otherwise have?*

4. *What steps could you take to build unlikely relationships with people who would benefit from access to your ideas, opportunities and resources?*

Conclusion

Community, city and country transformation is led by people who pioneer rather than people who settle. As the Apple advert said, 'Here's to the crazy ones. The misfits. The rebels. The troublemakers. The round pegs in the square holes. The ones who see things differently. They're not fond of rules. And they have no respect for the status quo. You can quote them, disagree with them, glorify or vilify them. About the only thing you can't do is ignore them. Because they change things. They push the human race forward. And while some may see them as the crazy ones, we see genius. Because the people who are crazy enough to think they can change the world, are the ones who do.'

The kind of faith that brings about transformation is not safe and domesticated, it is wild and adventurous. Abraham, even at his ripe age, was called by God to pack up his home and set off on an adventure. God promised him great things but didn't tell him where he was going or how he was going to get there (Genesis 12). It was a massive faith adventure. Whilst we might feel settled and comfortable right now there is always the possibility that God may call us, whatever our age, to make changes that change our world and change the world.

There is always the temptation to domesticate our faith, to make it safe and comfortable, by constantly reducing and removing risks. Our faith can become de-risked by living within what we know we can do, by setting goals we know we can achieve and by living within the resources we know we have. The danger is then that our faith reaches a point where it is no longer faith at all because we have removed any uncertainly about what might happen and therefore the need for reliance on God. It's when we step beyond our own knowledge, our own experience and our own ability that we know that what is happening is God!

In this book I wanted to ask a double barrelled question, "What is God doing and how do we join in?" In each chapter I have highlighted something that I think God is doing to bring about transformation and asked questions about how we can get involved:

1. De-Privatising Faith – Where is God moving his people to engage in civic life?

2. God's Transformation Strategy – Where is God leading his people to unconditionally and sacrificially love others?

3. Stronger Together – Where is God helping his

Church to find one another and recognise the strength they have as one rather than as many?

4. Prayer Rising – Where is God growing the volume and intensity of prayer for transformation?

5. Social Action – Where is God increasing his people's social consciousness and social action to help those people most at need?

6. Cultural Change – Where is God leading his people to view their work as worship, and their workplace as the context for his transformation?

7. Talking Jesus – Where is God growing his people's confidence to be bold and courageous to talk about Jesus to others?

8. Good Community – Where is God developing a vision for what change and transformation look like?

9. Participative Society – Where is God building nations of people with a great commitment to social responsibility?

10. Numbers Speak Louder Than Words – Where is God helping his Church speak in numbers as well as stories in order to communicate the value of what it does?

11. Salt and Pepper – Where is God building multi-ethnic relationships to increase diversity?

12. Distinctive Faiths – Where is God building true and honest relationships between followers of Jesus and people of other faiths?

13. Outrageous Generosity – Where is God leading people to be ultra-generous with their finances and resources?

14. Unlikely Relationships – Where is God connecting unlikely people in order to do something new?

All pioneers and adventurers need to understand the times they are living in and have a sense of their direction of travel. I pray that these fourteen indicators, where I sense there is holy energy, will help you understand the times and provide a sense of direction. They are like the sensitive needle of a compass, which is constantly changing and adjusting to point you in the direction of true north.

There are a number of ways that you can use these fourteen indicators, they could include:

- Personal reflection
- Small group discussion
- Leadership team study
- Sunday talks
- Marketplace groups

What single step could you take today to use this book to help yourself and others take a further step to join what God is doing? Exercise adventurous faith rather than a domesticated faith and see what more God may do in you, through you and because of you.

ABOUT THE AUTHOR

Matt Bird is an international speaker, author and broadcaster who is passionate about building life-transforming relationships across communities, cities and countries. He has spoken in more than thirty nations to more than a million people. He is the author of ten books, writes for *The Times* newspaper and hosts a show on TBN TV. www.mattbirdspeaker.com

Matt is the founder of Cinnamon Network which helps churches transform communities. It is best known for identifying and incubating the replication of church based community projects to national scale and helping the church partner effectively with civic organisations.

Cinnamon research has valued the time given by the UK Church to their communities as worth £3 billion every year. www.cinnamonnetwork.co.uk

He is also the founder of Relationology, a unique approach to client-centric business development through the power of relationships. His clients include the big four professional services firms, private banks and luxury goods businesses. www.relationology.co.uk

Matt lives in Wimbledon, UK with his wife Esther and their three children.